TABLE OF C[ONTENTS]

. . . .

Introduction

*D*o you sometimes wonder, as I have, how career decisions are made? Are they spontaneous, long in coming, or even far different from anything one had imagined? I have been writing biographies seeking answers from successful men and women in many cultures and many different kinds of professions—artists, writers, political activists, performers, and scientists.

My first book for young readers was about New York City's popular mayor Fiorello La Guardia, son of Italian immigrants, who was a fighter pilot during World War I, helped immigrants when they arrived on Ellis Island, and fought against corrupt city politicians.

My books on Charles Chaplin, Edward Lear, Rudyard Kipling, and Fanny Mendelssohn began with reading their autobiographies and personal letters. I was sometimes astounded by the problems they overcame during childhood and as young adults. During Chaplin's childhood it was extreme poverty. He left school and *went to work as an eight-year-old when his single mother was sent to a mental institution. Lear, one of twenty children, was born with epilepsy and would have been institutionalized were it not for his older sister's help. While his parents were in India, Kipling was sent to live with strangers in Britain, who frequently punished him for being a dull, lazy student, when in fact it was bad eyesight that made him a poor reader. Composer Fanny Mendelssohn's attempt to become a serious composer like her brother was thwarted by her family and the stigma against women in the arts. I've read more than forty autobiographies, choosing to represent individuals whose stories are most compelling for this book, whose persistence, self-confidence, and talent have led them toward success. I also included some inspiring pieces written just for this book. Obviously there is no one formula for success, but learning how others coped and succeeded should send its own message to readers of this book.*

—Gloria Kamen

WRITERS

What does one need to become a writer? A good use of language, imagination, fresh ideas? For each of the writers in this section, the decision to make writing a lifelong career was triggered by the discovery that writing was what he or she most wanted to do.

Introduction to

Russell Baker

The advice, or perhaps the correct word is *command*, that Russell Baker heard and hated when he was a boy was to work hard and to not be lazy. "Buddy," his mother would say, "you need to make something of yourself." His mother's definition of making something of himself allowed for only two choices: success in business or as a railroad man like his stepfather.

"Buddy" was brought up by his widowed mother and a host of relatives, first in the backwoods of Virginia, then, during the Depression years, in the city of Baltimore. His first display of *gumption*, another of his mother's favorite words, was selling copies of *The Saturday Evening Post* door-to-door at age eight.

It was in the year before high school graduation that the possibility of becoming a writer first entered his mind.

Baker, through his regular "Observer" column in *The New York Times*, would far surpass his mother's definition of "making something of himself." *The New York Times* ran his column for years, and in 1979 he was given a Pulitzer Prize for distinguished commentary. Four years later Baker was awarded another Pulitzer for his autobiography, *Growing Up*, the book from which this excerpt is taken. His other collections of popular essays and columns include *Poor Russell's Almanac* and *So This Is Depravity*.

Russell Baker

from Growing Up

The only thing that truly interested me was writing, and I knew that sixteen-year-olds did not come out of high school and become writers. I thought of writing as something to be done only by the rich. It was so obviously not real work, not a job at which you could earn a living. Still, I had begun to think of myself as a writer. It was the only thing for which I seemed to have the smallest talent, and, silly though it sounded when I told people I'd like to be a writer, it gave me a way of thinking about myself which satisfied my need to have an identity.

The notion of becoming a writer had flickered off and on in my head since the Belleville days, but it wasn't until my third year in high school that the possibility took hold. Until then I'd been bored by everything associated with English courses. I found English grammar dull and baffling. I hated the assignments to turn out "compositions," and went at them like heavy labor, turning out leaden, lackluster paragraphs that were agonies for teachers to read and for me to write. The classics thrust on me to read seemed as deadening as chloroform.

When our class was assigned to Mr. Fleagle for third-year English I anticipated another grim year in that dreariest of subjects. Mr. Fleagle was notorious among City students for dullness and inability to inspire. He was said to be stuffy, dull, and hopelessly out of date. To me he looked to be sixty or seventy and prim to a fault. He wore primly severe eyeglasses, his wavy hair was primly cut and primly combed. He wore prim vested suits with neckties blocked primly against the collar buttons of his primly starched white shirts. He had a primly pointed jaw, a primly straight nose, and a prim manner of speaking that was so correct, so gentlemanly, that he seemed a comic antique.

I anticipated a listless, unfruitful year with Mr. Fleagle and for a long time was not disappointed. We read *Macbeth*. Mr. Fleagle loved *Macbeth* and wanted us to love it too, but he lacked the gift of infecting others with his own passion. He tried to convey the murderous ferocity of Lady Macbeth one day by reading aloud the passage that concludes:

I have given suck, and know
How tender 'tis to love the babe that milks me.
I would, while it was smiling in my face,
Have plucked my nipple from his boneless gums.

The idea of prim Mr. Fleagle plucking his nipple from boneless gums was too much for the class. We burst into gasps of irrepressible snickering. Mr. Fleagle stopped.

"There is nothing funny, boys, about giving suck to a babe. It is the—the very essence of motherhood, don't you see."

He constantly sprinkled his sentences with "don't you see." It wasn't a question but an exclamation of mild surprise at our ignorance. "Your pronoun needs an antecedent, don't you see," he would say, very primly. "The purpose of the Porter's scene, boys, is to provide comic relief from the horror, don't you see."

Late in the year we tackled the informal essay. "The essay, don't you see, is the . . ." My mind went numb. Of all forms of writing, none seemed so boring as the essay. Naturally we would have to write informal essays. Mr. Fleagle distributed a homework sheet offering us a choice of topics. None was quite so simpleminded as "What I Did on My Summer Vacation," but most seemed to be almost as dull. I took the list home and dawdled until the night before the essay was due. Sprawled on the sofa, I finally faced up to the grim task, took the list out of my notebook, and scanned it. The topic on which my eye stopped was "The Art of Eating Spaghetti."

This title produced an extraordinary sequence of mental images. Surging up out of the depths of memory came a vivid recollection of a night in Belleville when all of us were seated around the supper table—Uncle Allen, my mother, Uncle Charlie, Doris, Uncle Hal—and Aunt Pat served spaghetti for supper. Spaghetti was an exotic treat in those days. Neither

Doris nor I had ever eaten spaghetti, and none of the adults had enough experience to be good at it. All the good humor of Uncle Allen's house reawoke in my mind as I recalled the laughing arguments we had that night about the socially respectable method for moving spaghetti from plate to mouth.

Suddenly I wanted to write about that, about the warmth and good feeling of it, but I wanted to put it down simply for my own joy, not for Mr. Fleagle. It was a moment I wanted to recapture and hold for myself. I wanted to relive the pleasure of an evening at New Street. To write it as I wanted, however, would violate all the rules of formal composition I'd learned in school, and Mr. Fleagle would surely give it a failing grade. Never mind. I would write something else for Mr. Fleagle after I had written this thing for myself.

When I finished it the night was half gone and there was no time left to compose a proper, respectable essay for Mr. Fleagle. There was no choice next morning but to turn in my private reminiscence of Belleville. Two days passed before Mr. Fleagle returned the graded papers, and he returned everyone's but mine. I was bracing myself for a command to report to Mr. Fleagle immediately after school for discipline when I saw him lift my paper from his desk and rap for the class's attention.

"Now, boys," he said, "I want to read you an essay. This is titled 'The Art of Eating Spaghetti.' "

And he started to read. My words! He was reading *my words* out loud to the entire class. What's more, the entire class was listening. Listening attentively. Then somebody laughed, then the entire class was laughing, and not in contempt and ridicule, but with openhearted enjoyment. Even Mr. Fleagle stopped two or three times to repress a small prim smile.

I did my best to avoid showing pleasure, but what I was feeling was pure ecstasy at this startling demonstration that my words had the power to make people laugh. In the eleventh grade, at the eleventh hour as it were, I had discovered a calling. It was the happiest moment of my entire school career. When Mr. Fleagle finished he put the final seal on my happiness by saying, "Now that, boys, is an essay, don't you see. It's—don't you see—it's of the very essence of the essay, don't you see. Congratulations, Mr. Baker."

For the first time, light shone on a possibility. It wasn't a very heartening possibility, to be sure. Writing couldn't lead to a job after high school, and it was hardly honest work, but Mr. Fleagle had opened a door for me. After that I ranked Mr. Fleagle among the finest teachers in the school.

My mother was almost as delighted as I when I showed her Mr. Fleagle's A-plus and described my triumph. Hadn't she always said I had a talent for writing? "Now if you work hard at it, Buddy, you can make something of yourself."

Introduction to

Katherine Paterson

*O*ne *of my professors asked me if I'd ever thought of becoming
a writer. I was astounded. I'd spent my life reading. I knew what
good writing was. "No," I said, "I wouldn't want to add another
mediocre writer to the world." "Well, perhaps," she said, "that is
what God is calling you to be."*

Katherine Paterson's response years later was to become an
excellent writer.

When young Katherine arrived from China to live in
Richmond, Virginia, and a year later in Winston-Salem, North
Carolina, she became the quintessential outsider with a slight
British accent, coming from somewhere "out there" in Asia,
and wearing secondhand clothes that were totally out of style
with her new classmates'. As if that weren't enough, her family
moved eighteen times by the time she was eighteen. All this
would have been daunting for most children, but Katherine
not only survived but used her unusual background to her

advantage by writing some of the best-loved children's books: *The Sign of the Chrysanthemum*, *The Master Puppeteer*, *Jacob Have I Loved*, and *The Tale of the Mandarin Duck*, to name just a few. To date she has written thirty books and garnered the most prestigious awards of any current writer of children's books, including two National Book Awards, two Newbery Medals, the Scott O'Dell Award for Historical Fiction, the international Hans Christian Andersen Medal for Writing in 1998, the New York Public Library award, also in 1998, and the Governor's Award for the State of Vermont, where she now lives.

Her many honorary degrees have come from colleges around the United States.

Several of her books have been made into plays: "Bridge to Terabithia," "The Tale of the Mandarin Duck," and "The Great Gilly Hopkins."

Almost all of Paterson's books have a hopeful, positive message, a reflection of the person she is, the life she's achieved, and the understanding she has of young people throughout today's world who hope for a better life.

Katherine Paterson

From On Becoming a Writer

I'm always a bit embarrassed when a young reader asks, "Mrs. Paterson, when did you first know that you wanted to be a writer?" I can tell by her earnestness that this nine-year-old is already well on the way to a literary career. The fact is that I never wanted to be a writer, at least not when I was a child or even as a young woman. Today I very much want to be a writer, but when I was nine or ten, I wanted to be either a movie star or a missionary. When I was twenty, I wanted to get married and have lots of children.

For as long as I can remember, I wanted to be a reader. I was born in China and was noisily bilingual by the time I was two. My parents were Presbyterian missionaries, and we lived in the city of Huai'an, where there were no English bookstores or libraries. So the only English books available were those in our small family library. We were fortunate, though. Our mother loved to read to us, so my earliest memories are tied up with the comforting lavender smell of my mother as I pressed my small body as close to hers as possible and thrilled with horror at the idea of "James James Morrison Morrison Weatherby George Dupree's" delinquent parent, who went casually strolling off to the end of the town and has never been heard of since. I suppose I am one of the few people in the world who hears Kipling in a soft Georgia accent. There was also Beatrix Potter and Robert Louis Stevenson and *Jo Boy*, a book nobody outside my family seems ever to have heard of. My mother's old kindergarten teacher back in Georgia had sent it to China so my mother could share it with her children. I don't kill spiders because of *Jo Boy*, nor do I sweep down spiderwebs, in case any acquaintance thinks it's poor housekeeping. I can still almost recite from heart the poems and stories of A. A. Milne, and I loved *The Wind in the Willows* almost as fanatically as the youth of the sixties loved Tolkien.

Because I loved reading so, I taught myself how to read long before I entered school and Dick and Jane imposed their stifling weight upon my eager little spirit. Which may explain the source of my first published work, which appeared in the Shanghai American School newspaper when I was about seven:

Pat, pat, pat.
There is the cat.
Where is the rat?
Pat, pat, pat.

Alongside my effort was a note from the second-grade teacher that read, "The second graders' work is not up to our usual standards this week because we were too busy working on the circus." Thus my first published work ran side by side with my first critical review. I was well warned.

Fortunately, very few samples of my early writing survived the eighteen moves I made before I was eighteen years old. There is, however, one rather nice letter I wrote to my father the same year that I wrote "Pat, Pat, Pat." Because China was at war with Japan, the family had to stay in Shanghai, but my intrepid father was back at work in our old hometown, Huai'an, even as it was being invaded. The letter I wrote is childlike. Still, it is full of human feeling, a piece of writing I am not ashamed of to this day. But then, I knew my father loved me and would accept with pleasure any effort. It took me a long time to trust teachers to this degree.

In December of 1940, American families were ordered out of China. We had been refugees once before in 1937, so I had been to the States, though I had been a foreigner in the land my parents called home. Among the more than twice-told tales in my family is the tragic one about the year we lived in Richmond, Virginia, when I came home from first grade on February 14 without a single valentine. My mother grieved over this event until her death, asking me once why I didn't write a story about the time I didn't get any valentines. "But Mother," I said, "*all* my stories are about the time I didn't get any valentines."

I was asked some years ago by a parent how she could encourage her son to become a writer. I couldn't imagine what to say in reply. Have him born in a foreign country, start a war that drives him not once, but twice like a refugee to another land where his clothes, his speech, his very thoughts will cut him off from his peers. Then, perhaps, he will begin to read books for comfort and invent elaborate fantasies inside his head for entertainment. Actually, I kept my mouth shut. I don't believe for one minute that her son needed to experience what I've experienced in order to write books. I'm sure there are many fine writers who have overcome the disadvantages of a normal childhood and gone on to do great things. It's just that we weird little kids do seem to have a leg up.

When I enrolled in the Calvin H. Wiley School in Winston-Salem, North Carolina, I was nine years old, small for my age, on the inside a show-off of cosmic proportions, on the outside a prototype of timidity. I spoke English, as my friends in Shanghai had, with a British accent and wore secondhand clothing that my classmates recognized as their own donations to charity. Because children are somewhat vague about geography, and my classmates knew only that I had come from somewhere over there, they decided I was, if not a Japanese spy, certainly suspect. The only thing I could do anything about was the accent. So although since that time I have lived in seven states and another foreign country, I still speak like someone from the Piedmont in North Carolina.

My accent is not the only thing I owe to Calvin H. Wiley

School. On the playground of Wiley School I spent some of the most miserable hours of my young life. This was largely because of a well-developed seventh-grade girl named Pansy, who with her gang of seventh-grade Amazons roamed the playground in search of victims to bully. I couldn't have been much of a challenge, and, to be truthful, they never laid a finger on me. They just leered and threatened. I would spot them coming across the great expanse of the grounds and be reduced to jelly.

I can't remember at what point the library became my sanctuary. I don't even remember the librarian's name. What I do remember was her manner, which was cheerful and precise. I stayed in Wiley School for almost three and a half years—a record tenure—and as I got older, I was arranging cards in the card catalog, opening the new books, carefully, a bit at a time, and gently pressing back the pages, pasting the pockets in the back. I was even allowed, eventually, to mend books. The librarian taught me how to put on the double cloth binding, dipping the brush into the large pot of glue, pulling it against the edge of the pot, first one side of the brush, then the other, so no errant drops would remain to fall upon the precious book. Years later it was a scene that found its way, transformed, into the opening pages of my novel *The Master Puppeteer*. I still marvel at this woman, as fastidious as she was, entrusting us children with the care of her books. I have never taken more pride in any job I have held than I took in being a library aide at Calvin H. Wiley School. I am sure that my sensuous love for books as paper, ink, and binding—treasures to be respected and cherished—is in large part because of the Wiley School librarian.

My aborted writing career had a second spurt of life at Wiley School. It was not because we had instruction in creative writing. Nothing that frivolous would have been allowed. "Writing" was the class when you learned to do the swirls and slants of Palmer Penmanship. But as I grew more comfortable in this strange land of America, the hidden show-off side of my nature began to crack the shell of timidity. I longed to be, of all things, an actress, and the only way to act was to write plays for my classmates and me to act out on the playground. I achieved a tiny bit of fame when I was in seventh grade and the teacher allowed us to act out one of my playground dramas in the classroom. I had wisely given it a historical setting, which made it somehow related to real schoolwork.

Five years and six schools later I entered a small Presbyterian college in Bristol, Tennessee. I discovered that if you declared for an English major, you got to read almost all the time. I hadn't realized how much you had to write. My tiny West Virginia high school hadn't taught me how to write anything, much less a term paper. So the first time I got the assignment to write a research paper was in the first semester of my sophomore year, when I had six of them due at once. I learned fast. It was my college English professors who first praised my writing, but I was reading Shakespeare and Donne and Gerard Manley Hopkins. How could I regard term papers as works of serious literary merit?

My dream of becoming a movie star never came true, but I continued to do a lot of acting through high school and college, even writing a one-act play that one of my professors sent off to a drama critic she knew. The critic was polite, but patronizing. It was, he said, not too bad for a student project.

On my way to becoming a missionary, I spent a year teaching in a rural school in northern Virginia. I never forgot that wonderful class, and the area where they lived became the setting for my novel *Bridge to Terabithia*.

After Lovettsville I spent two years at a Presbyterian graduate school in Richmond, Virginia, studying Bible and Christian education. One of my professors stopped me in the hall one day and asked if I'd ever thought of being a writer. I was astounded. I'd spent my life reading. I knew what good writing was. "No," I said, "I wouldn't want to add another mediocre writer to the world."

"Well, perhaps," she said, "that is what God is calling you to be." It took me several years to realize what she was saying: that if I didn't dare to be mediocre, I'd never be anything at all.

My childhood dream had been to become, like my parents, a missionary to China and eat Chinese food three times a day. But China was closed to Americans in 1957, and a Japanese friend at the seminary urged me to go to Japan instead. I remembered the Japanese as the enemy. They were the ones who dropped the bombs and then occupied the cities where I had lived as a child. I was afraid of the Japanese, and so I hated them. But my trusted friend persuaded me to put aside those childish feelings and give myself a chance to view the Japanese in a new way.

I came to love Japan in the four years I lived there. I spent the first two years in language school and the next two working with rural pastors on the island of Shikoku. I was the only English-speaking person in the town where I lived, but the people I lived among and worked with made me feel very much at home. I had every intention of spending the rest of my life in Japan, but when I returned to the States for a year of study at Union Seminary in New York City, I met a young Presbyterian pastor who changed the direction of my life once again. We were married in 1962 and soon began to fulfill that other ambition—to have lots of children.

My life as a writer really began in 1964. The professor who had dared me to be a writer got me a writing assignment. Because of her urging the Presbyterian Church asked me to write a book for fifth and sixth graders. Since the denomination had given me the scholarship to study, and I had married instead of going back to Japan, I felt that I owed them something for their money. So I began to write. By the time the book was published, I had moved three times, acquired three children, and was hooked on writing.

But I decided I didn't want to write nonfiction. I wanted to write what I most loved to read—fiction. I didn't know that wanting to write fiction and being able to write publishable fiction were two quite different things. In four years we had four children—two adopted and two homemade—and in the cracks of time between feedings, diapering, cooking, reading aloud, walking to the park, and carpooling to nursery school, I wrote and wrote and published nothing.

A friend felt sorry for me. There I was with all these children, trying to write, with no success. She decided to take me to an adult education course in creative writing one night a week. Five years and many rejections later, the novel I wrote, a chapter a week for a class in writing for children, was published. I had, at last, become a writer.

Introduction to

Isaac Asimov

Here in his own words is how Isaac Asimov defined his career as a writer: *Although I have written over a hundred and twenty books, on almost every subject from astronomy to Shakespeare and from mathematics to satire, it is probably as a science fiction writer that I am best known.*

Asimov was born in 1920 in New York City into a family that, as he said, was "too poor to afford books." He was, nevertheless, a ravenous reader. From an early age he discovered and used that magical little thing called a library card, and began writing science fiction stories while still in high school.

In his book, *The Early Asimov, or Eleven Years of Trying,* Asimov tells of his astonishment when his brazen, unscheduled, first interview with a magazine editor went well. He recalls the exact date, June 21, 1938, of his meeting with John Campbell, having just completed high school. Asimov was eighteen.

Isaac Asimov

*from The Early Asimov, or
Eleven Years of Trying*

I began to write when I was very young—eleven, I think. The reasons are obscure. I might say it was the result of an unreasoning urge, but that would just indicate I could think of no reason.

Perhaps it was because I was an avid reader in a family that was too poor to afford books, even the cheapest, and besides, a family that considered cheap books unfit reading. I had to go to the library (my first library card was obtained for me by my father when I was six years old) and make do with two books per week.

This was simply not enough, and my craving drove me to extremes. At the beginning of each school term, I eagerly read through every schoolbook I was assigned, going from cover to cover like a personified conflagration. Since I was blessed with a tenacious memory and with instant recall, that was all the studying I had to do for *that* school term, but I was through before the week was over, and then what?

So, when I was eleven, it occurred to me that if I wrote my own books, I could then reread them at my leisure. I never really wrote a complete book, of course. I would start one and keep rambling on with it till I outgrew it and then I would start another. All these early writings are forever gone, though I remember some of the details quite clearly.

In the spring of 1934 I took a special English course given at my high school (Boys' High School in Brooklyn), that placed the accent on writing. The teacher was also faculty adviser for the semiannual literary magazine put out by the students, and it was his intention to gather material. I took that course.

It was a humiliating experience. I was fourteen at the time, and a rather green and innocent fourteen. I wrote trifles, while everyone else in the class (who were sixteen apiece) wrote sophisticated, tragic mood pieces. All of them made no particular secret of their scorn for me, and though I resented it bitterly there was nothing I could do about it.

For a moment I thought I had them when one of my products was accepted for the semiannual literary magazine while many of theirs were rejected. Unfortunately the teacher told me, with callous insensitivity, that mine was the only item submitted that was humorous and that since he had to have *one* nontragic piece he was forced to take it.

It was called "Little Brothers," dealt with the arrival of my own little brother five years earlier, and was my first piece of published material of any kind. I suppose it can be located in the records at Boys' High, but I don't have it.

Sometimes I wonder what happened to all those great tragic writers in the class. I don't remember a single name and I have no intention of ever trying to find out—but I sometimes wonder.

It was not until May 29, 1937 (according to a date I once jotted down—though that was before I began my diary, so I won't swear to it), that the vague thought occurred to me that I ought to write something for professional publication; something that would be *paid for*! Naturally it would have to be a science fiction story, for I had been an avid science fiction fan since 1929 and I recognized no other form of literature as in any way worthy of my efforts.

The story I began to compose for the purpose, the first story I ever wrote with a view to becoming a "writer," was entitled "Cosmic Corkscrew."

In it I viewed time as a helix (that is, something like a bed-spring). Someone could cut across from one turn directly to the next, thus moving into the future by some exact interval but being incapable of traveling one day less into the future. My protagonist made the cut across time and found the Earth deserted. All animal life was gone; yet there was every sign that life had existed until very shortly before—and no indication at all of what had brought about the disappearance. It was told in the first person from a lunatic asylum, because the narrator had, of course, been placed in a madhouse after he returned and tried to tell his tale.

I wrote only a few pages in 1937, then lost interest. The mere fact that I had publication in mind must have paralyzed me. As long as something I wrote was intended for my own eyes only, I could be carefree enough. The thought of possible other readers weighed down heavily upon my every word. So I abandoned it.

Then, in May 1938, the most important magazine in the field, *Astounding Science Fiction*, changed its publication schedule from the third Wednesday of the month to the fourth Friday. When the June issue did not arrive on its accustomed day, I went into a decline.

By May 17, I could stand it no more and took the subway to 79 Seventh Avenue, where the publishing house, Street & Smith Publications, Inc., was then located. There, an official of the firm informed me of the changed schedule, and on May 19, the June issue arrived.

The near brush with doom, and the ecstatic relief that followed, reactivated my desire to write and publish. I returned to "Cosmic Corkscrew" and by June 19 it was finished.

The next question was what to do with it. I had absolutely no idea what one did with a manuscript intended for publication, and no one I knew had any idea either. I discussed it with my father, whose knowledge of the real world was scarcely greater than my own, and he had no idea either.

But then it occurred to me that, the month before, I had gone to 79 Seventh Avenue merely to inquire about the nonappearance of *Astounding*. I had not been struck by lightning for doing so. Why not repeat the trip, then, and hand in the manuscript in person?

The thought was a frightening one. It became even more frightening when my father further suggested that necessary preliminaries included a shave and my best suit. That meant I would have to take additional time, and the day was already wearing on and I would have to be back in time to make the afternoon newspaper delivery. (My father had a candy store and newsstand, and life was very complicated in those days for a creative writer of artistic and sensitive bent such as myself. For instance, we lived in an apartment in which all the rooms were in a line and the only way of getting from the living room to the bedroom of my parents, or of my sister, or of my brother, was by going through *my* bedroom. My bedroom was therefore frequently gone through, and the fact that I might be in the throes of creation meant nothing to anyone.)

I compromised. I shaved, but did not bother changing suits, and off I went. The date was June 21, 1938.

I was convinced that, for daring to ask to see the editor of *Astounding Science Fiction*, I would be thrown out of the building bodily, and that my manuscript would be torn up and thrown out after me in a shower of confetti. My father, however (who had lofty notions) was convinced that a writer—by which he meant anyone with a manuscript— would be treated with the respect due an intellectual. He had no fears at all—but I was the one who had to go into the building.

Trying to mask panic, I asked to see the editor. The girl behind the desk (I can see the scene in my mind's eye right now exactly as it was) spoke briefly on the phone and said, "Mr. Campbell will see you."

She directed me through a large, loftlike room filled with huge rolls of paper and enormous piles of magazines and permeated with the heavenly smell of pulp (a smell that, to this day, will recall my youth in aching detail and reduce me to tears of nostalgia). And there, in a small room on the other side, was Mr. Campbell.

John Wood Campbell, Jr., had been working for Street & Smith for a year and had taken over sole command of *Astounding Stories* (which he had promptly renamed *Astounding Science Fiction*) a couple of months earlier. He was only twenty-eight years old then. Under his own name and under his pen name, Don A. Stuart, he was one of the most famous and highly regarded authors of science fiction, but he was about to bury his writing reputation forever under the far greater renown he was to gain as editor.

He was to remain editor of *Astounding Science Fiction* and of its successor, *Analog Science Fact—Science Fiction*, for a third of a century. During all that time, he and I were to remain friends, but however old I grew and however venerable and respected a star of our mutual field I was to become, I never approached him with anything but that awe he inspired in me on the occasion of our first meeting.

He was a large man, an opinionated man, who smoked and

talked constantly, and who enjoyed, above anything else, the production of outrageous ideas, which he bounced off his listener and dared him to refute. It was difficult to refute Campbell even when his ideas were absolutely and madly illogical.

We talked for over an hour that first time. He showed me forthcoming issues of the magazine (actual *future* issues in the cellulose-flesh). I found he had printed a fan letter of mine in the issue about to be published, and another in the next—so he knew the genuineness of my interest.

He told me about himself, about his pen name and about his opinions. He told me that his father had sent in one of his manuscripts to *Amazing Stories* when he was seventeen and that it would have been published but the magazine lost it and he had no carbon. (I was ahead of him there. I had brought in the story myself and I had a carbon.) He also promised to read my story that night and to send a letter, whether acceptance or rejection, the next day. He promised also that in case of rejection he would tell me what was wrong with it so I could improve.

He lived up to every promise. Two days later, on June 23, I heard from him. It was a rejection. (Since this book deals with real events and is not a fantasy—you can't be surprised that my first story was instantly rejected.)

Here is what I said in my diary about the rejection:

"At 9:30 I received back 'Cosmic Corkscrew' with a polite letter of rejection. He didn't like the slow beginning, the suicide at the end."

Campbell also didn't like the first-person narration and the stiff dialog, and further pointed out that the length (nine thousand words) was inconvenient—too long for a short story, too short for a novelette. Magazines had to be put together like jigsaw puzzles, you see, and certain lengths for individual stories were more convenient than others.

By that time, though, I was off and running. The joy of having spent an hour and more with John Campbell, the thrill of talking face-to-face and on even terms with an idol, had already filled me with the ambition to write another science fiction story, better than the first, so that I could try him again. The pleasant letter of rejection—two full pages—in which he discussed my story seriously and with no trace of patronization or contempt, reinforced my joy. Before June 23 was over, I was halfway through the first draft of another story.

Many years later I asked Campbell (with whom I had by then grown to be on the closest terms) why he had bothered with me at all, since that first story was surely utterly impossible.

"It was," he said frankly, for he never flattered. "On the other hand, I saw something in *you*. You were eager and you listened, and I knew you wouldn't quit no matter how many rejections I handed you. As long as you were willing to work hard at improving, I was willing to work with you."

That was John. I wasn't the only writer, whether newcomer or old-timer, that he was to work with in this fashion.

Patiently, and out of his own enormous vitality and talent, he built up a stable of the best science fiction writers the world had, 'till then, ever seen.

What happened to "Cosmic Corkscrew" after that I don't really know. I abandoned it and never submitted it anywhere else.

Introduction to

Julia Alvarez

Ever since I became a published writer, my family has been trying to figure out where the writing talent came from. The Espaillats have always been poets, one uncle (on the Espaillat side) noted. Another uncle believes that I probably got the writing genes from my father's side of the family.

Vermont writer Julia Alvarez, born in the Dominican Republic in 1950, lived a comfortable lifestyle there with her educated parents, three sisters, and large extended family until her father came under suspicion of trying to overthrow the repressive dictatorship of Rafael Trujillo.

In her book of autobiographical essays titled *Something to Declare*, Alvarez describes her family's fortunate escape to the United States when she turned ten. It was then, in her new environment, that she considered the possibility of becoming a writer. But the process was not easy.

In her book of essays Alvarez describes the years of struggle before finding her own direction and writing style that led to a successful career as a writer and teacher.

Alvarez has written a number of best-selling novels including: *How the Garcia Girls Lost Their Accents*, *In the Time of the Butterflies*, and *Yo!*

She has taught creative writing at the University of Illinois, George Washington University, Middlebury College, and the Bread Loaf Writers' Conference, and is a regular speaker at writers' conferences around the country.

Julia Alvarez

from Something to Declare

Once upon a time, I lived in another country and in another language under a cruel dictatorship, which my father was plotting to overthrow. But what I remember is not the cruel dictator, not the disappearances, nor my parents' nervous voices behind closed doors, but the storybook that helped me get through the long, dull school days that were my understanding of what dictatorships made children do.

I lay on my stomach under my bed, a six-, seven-, eight-, nine-, ten-year-old girl—this went on for a long time, as long times do during childhood. With the bedskirt providing a perfect cover, I felt as if I had actually been transported to a silken tent in a faraway country with nothing but my wits to keep me alive. The storybook I was reading was one that my maiden aunt Tití, the only reader I knew, had given me. *The Thousand and One Nights*, it was called, and on its cover sat a young girl with a veil over her long, dark hair and beside her,

reclining on one elbow and
was a young man with a tu
about this young girl was that
other storybooks, Scheherazade
girl: dark-haired, almond-eyed, w

This book was the only voluntary
poor student and poorly behaved. In
the truth, the reason I was hiding und   early in the
morning instead of reading my book openly on top of my bed
was to avoid having to go to school that day.

Every morning after breakfast my mother and aunts rounded
up my sisters and cousins for the drive to school. There was a
crowd of us—three cars were needed—and by the time one car
was filled up and on its way, the aunts weren't quite sure who
had already gone and who was left to transport. So, if I slipped
away from my sisters and cousins, and hightailed it to my
bedroom, and threw myself under the bed, and stayed there,
quietly reading my book of stories, it would not be until
midday, when the school crowd returned for *la comida del
mediodía*, that my mother realized that I had played hooky
again right under her very nose.

Why did I do this? School was deadly. I thought I would
surely die of boredom sitting on that hard chair listening to
Mrs. Brown talk about the pilgrims or *i* before *e* or George
Washington cutting down a cherry tree. We were attending the
Carol Morgan School because my parents had decided that we
should learn English and get "an American education" rather

e. To this day, they claim this choice
on to the United States so much easier. But
they have known back then that we would be going
xile in a few years?

So what I was learning in school had nothing to do with the lush, tropical, and dangerous world around me. We were living in a dictatorship, complete with spies, late-night disappearences, torture, and death. What, indeed, did this world have to do with the capital of Alabama and Dick and Jane and a big red bouncing ball? And what on earth was apple pie? Was it anything at all like a *pastel de tamarindo*? No wonder I shut the doors to my attention and refused to do my homework. My education was a colonialist one: not imposed from the outside but from within my own family. I was to learn the culture, tongue and manners of the powerful country to our north that had set our dictator in place and kept him there for thirty-one years. Maybe my parents did know what they were doing.

And maybe, I, sensing the unspoken world of intrigue and danger around me, where El Jefe ruled supreme, found kinship with the girl on the cover of my storybook.

Certainly she had more to say to me than Dick and Jane.

I am Scheherazade, she would always begin. *I am a girl stuck in a kingdom that doesn't think females are very important.*

Why, that's just like me, I'd pipe up. It's always the boy cousins who are asked what they want to do with their lives.

Girls are told we are going to be wives and mothers. If we're asked at all, it's usually how many children we want and whom we might want to marry.

But even though I am a girl, Scheherazade went on, *I am ambitious and clever and I've found ways of getting around the restraints put upon me.*

Why, that's just like me, I put in. Here I am, hiding under this bed in the middle of a school day, doing what I please. And I've found other ways of getting around things as well. I can learn any poem by heart if I hear it read out loud a few times. When company comes, Mami dresses me up in my first communion dress and takes me out to recite in front of everyone. They reward me with *pesetas* and sometimes a whole *peso*. I've already told Mami that when I grow up, I'll go ahead and have those half-dozen babies I'm supposed to have, but I'm also going to become a famous actress who gets to travel around the world and do whatever she wants—

Very recently, I had a shock, Scheherazade interrupted. (*Pobrecita*, she could hardly get a word in edgewise!) *I found out that I am living in a country where our cruel sultan is killing all my girlfriends. First he marries them, then the next day he kills them. I've been racking my brains, trying to figure out a way to stop all this killing, and I think I've finally got a plan.*

Far off in the direction of the *palacio nacional*, a siren sounded. I wasn't sure what it meant. Sometimes the siren meant a "resignation," with the retiree appearing in the papers a few days later in a black-outlined box with a crucifix and

"Que descanse en paz" above a blurry photo of his face. Sometimes the siren meant our *jefe*, Rafael Leonidas Trujillo, was going out, and so the streets had to be cleared. I am sure that siren also meant other things my parents were afraid to tell me.

What I am going to do, Scheherazade confided, *is marry the sultan, and then, before he can kill me the next morning, I'm going to tell him a story.*

That's worked for me, I said, nodding at her bright-eyed face on the cover. Many, many times I had escaped punishment with a story. Just last week, Mami came rushing to find out who had broken my grandmother's blue crystal ball that sat on a pedestal under the tamarind tree. Of course, it seemed pretty obvious to her when she found my cousin Ique and me holding rakes, but I set her straight. I told Mami that the reason we were holding rakes was that we had just chased off the man who had broken the ball.

"And what man would that be?" my mother asked, eyes narrowed.

Hmm, I thought. What man would that be? I knew my parents were afraid of the *guardia* who periodically came on the property searching for an acquaintance or just asking for *un regalito* to buy their cigarillos. So, I explained that the man we had chased off was a *guardia* whom we had caught snooping around the property.

That sent a volley of terrified looks among the adults who had followed my mother outside at the sound of breaking

42

glass. How was I supposed to know that my father and uncles had joined the underground and were plotting the overthrow of the dictator? That my parents' seeming compliance was all show. That *guardia* on the grounds meant my family's participation had been uncovered. The adults went off in a cold sweat to a private conference behind locked doors while Ique and I were left to enjoy the tamarinds we had knocked down with our rakes.

So, early on, I learned that stories could save you. That stories could weave a spell even over powerful adults and get them off your case and on to other things like talking politics behind closed doors or making a tamarind *pastel* in the kitchen.

The power of stories was all around me, for the tradition of storytelling is deeply rooted in my Dominican culture. With over eighty percent illiteracy when I was growing up, the culture was still an oral culture. Rarely did I see anyone reading a book, except for my aunt Tití—and that was the reason, everyone knew, why she wasn't yet married. (She also wore pajamas and knew Latin, and read the dictionary, which didn't help.) Mostly people listened to radio programs and to each other. Streets were known, not by street signs, but by the stories or characters or events associated with them. The street where Chucho lives. You know, Chucho, the man born with a sixth finger on each hand because when his mother was pregnant, she stole a piece of *pudin de pan* from a neighbor, and so God punished her by putting an extra, shoplifting finger on her son's hands.

Ah yes, *that* Chucho, *that* street!

So it is no surprise, given my island oral tradition, that I became a storyteller. But it is still a surprise to me—given my nonliterary childhood, my aversion to writing and to anything that smacked of a classroom—that I grew up to write books and be a teacher.

Of course, what clinched it was an even bigger surprise, the surprise of my life, you could call it: escaping to the United States in August 1960, with the SIM (Military Intelligence Service) on my father's tail. Overnight, we lost everything: a homeland, an extended family, a culture, and yes, as I've already said, the language I felt at home in. The classroom English I had learned at Carol Morgan had very little to do with the English being spoken on the streets and in the playgrounds of New York City. I could not understand most things the Americans were saying to me with their marbles-in-their-mouths, fast-talking, elided American English, which Walt Whitman rightly termed "that barbaric yawp."

One thing I did understand: boys at school chased me across the playground, pelting me with stones, yelling, "Spic! Spic! Go back to where you came from!"

"No speak eengleesh," I lied, taking the easy way out, instead of being brave and speaking up like Scheherazade.

But my silence was also strategy. Inside my head a rich conversation had started, inspired by the world of books. Not

44

just *The Thousand and One Nights*, but Nancy Drew mysteries, *Little Women*, *Winnie the Pooh*. I was encouraged by teachers who asked me to write down what I remembered about that world I was so homesick for. I found that if I wrote down *the bright pink flowers in Mamita's garden*, I could summon up my grandmother's back patio with the hot-pink bougainvillea dropping down through the slats of the overhead trellis. By rubbing the lamp of language, I could make the genie appear: the sights, sounds, smells, the people and places of the homeland I had lost.

I realized something I had always known lying on my stomach under the bed: language was power. Written-down language was money in the bank.

Still, I remember the faces of those tormenting boys. The corners of their mouths were stained with egg yolk. Their eyes seemed colorless, without warmth or kindness. In their jeering voices I could hear some other voice—maybe a parent's—hurling the same kind of insults at them. I dreaded this playground gang because I could not speak *their* language clearly enough to make them understand that I was not their enemy.

"No speak eengleesh," they taunted my accent. "I'm Chiquita Banana and I'm here to say. . . ." They glared at me as if I were some repulsive creature with six fingers on *my* hands.

Sometimes the teacher caught them and gave them a talking-to or kept them after school. Finally, the pain of punishment must not have been worth the pleasure of watching me burst into tears, and they gave up picking on me and started in on someone else.

Looking back now, I can see that my path as a writer began in that playground. Somewhere inside, where we make promises to ourselves, I told myself I would learn English so well that Americans would sit up and notice. I told myself that one day I would express myself in a way that would make those boys feel bad they had tormented me. Yes, it was revenge that set me on the path of becoming a writer. At some point, though, revenge turned into redemption. Instead of pummeling those boys with my success, I began to want to save them. I wanted to change those looks of hate and mistrust, to transform the sultan's face into the beautiful face of the reclining prince on the cover of my childhood storybook.

Introduction to

Pauline Fisk

I can't remember a time when I wasn't making up stories and escaping into a world of my own.

From the time she was a young child, British author Pauline Fisk found that storytelling was a way of living within the restricted world of school and family—"in an age of ironed frocks and white socks, my hair in big bows, growing up into a teenager in an environment where 'developing a young woman's self' seemed to cause nothing but embarrassment."

From the age of nine Fisk was addicted to the wonderful tales of A. A. Milne, Enid Blyton, Hans Christian Andersen, and other classic writers. It was her affection for children's literature that set her on "the most important career decision in my life, to become an author—not when I grew up—but there and then."

She set out on a literary apprenticeship that carried on throughout her school life and beyond and finally came to its fulfillment after the birth of her fifth child, when, getting up at five every morning, she wrote her first novel for children, *Midnight Blue*. This was an immediate success, winning the Smarties Grand Prix in 1990 and being translated into six languages: Portuguese, German, Danish, Italian, Greek, and Japanese. A series of other novels followed: *Telling the Sea*, *Tyger Pool*, *The Beast of Whixall Moss*, *The Candle House*, and *The Secret of Sabrina Fludde*.

As a child, Fisk wrote stories and poems in the "voice" of authors she admired. Her inspiration now comes from the legends and history of the Welsh Marches, where she lives. But the voice she writes with is her own.

Pauline Fisk
Dreaming Big

A little-known fact about the Second World War is that the southern outpost of the British Isles was invaded and occupied by Nazi troops. My mother was a victim of this occupation, escaping from her Channel Island home across a mine-charged sea.

From her I inherited a sense of displacement, and a fear of water. The first was brought about by my mother's experiences as a refugee in London, and it profoundly affected the way that my brother and I were brought up. The second was attributable not only to the twenty-four hours she spent dodging mines in the English Channel, but to the suicide of her father. Missing the sea, which he had lived beside for most of his life, he drowned himself in six inches of water in a city duck pond.

My mother never recovered from the shock, and her grief and bitterness clouded my childhood. I didn't know what had happened until I found out as an adult, but I knew that something was wrong.

I'd look out at the rows of houses that hemmed in my childhood life, and know I didn't belong. I felt like a prisoner in a cage of streets and houses. I knew this wasn't really home—that I was born to be somewhere else.

Perhaps that sense of displacement is why I daydreamed so much, or perhaps I would have done it anyway. I have a photograph of myself aged three, peering over the garden wall. All that can be seen of me are a pair of eyes, a flash of white frock, and a row of Shirley Temple curls. What I was doing, my mother once explained, was telling stories to the big children who lived next door. I was little more than a toddler and they were at school, but they were asking, "What happened next?" and I was telling them.

I can't remember a time when I wasn't making up stories and escaping into a world of my own. My real-life world was tight and edgy, a dust-free crystal mausoleum of mirrors and glazed doors where nothing could be hidden apart from the secrets of the imagination. My mother was putting down new roots, striving to make herself a home, and everything in it had to be picture-postcard perfect—including me.

Old family photographs reveal the immaculate white frocks with starched bows in which my mother dressed me. I remember how stiff and scratchy they were, and how I longed to be a tomboy like the girls in Enid Blyton books. I wasn't allowed to play on grass for fear of getting dirty, wasn't allowed to wear jeans because they were "unladylike," and had to endure my hair being crimped in rows of tight little metal curlers while my mother swore my ramrod locks were natural.

Perhaps it was her past that made her want everything neat and tidy, or perhaps she was the product of her age. But I was different. I remember moving into a new house with a rambling wilderness of garden. I was thrilled, my four-year-old imagination running wild among its climbing roses, apple trees, trellises, and rockeries. But my mother made my father pull them all out and replace them with a tidy lawn that could be "managed properly."

I wasn't old enough to express in words the upset that I felt, but I was old enough to know that something special had been taken away. I hated my parents' new showcase lawn, and turned my attention—and my imagination—to the only wild places that remained: the back alleys and areas of scrubland between the rows of houses. Here, among brambles and flowering elders, dandelions and rambling columbines, I conjured up a world of mythic creatures who came out to play when no one was about; fairy folk and angelic beings whom I never actually saw—but I imagined that I could, and that was just as good!

In other words, my imagination gave me power. At home I might feel like a prisoner, seen by my parents as "willful," "difficult," and "rude," but inside my head I was free. I could be anyone I wanted, play with whom I liked, go where my fancy took me. And I did, too, running away inside my head to join the circus; becoming Heidi in her mountain hayloft; playing with Enid Blyton's Famous Five. I could even leave myself behind—junk that Pauline Fisk, and make up better heroines and heroes with more interesting stories and lives.

And I could write those stories down, and read them again. I remember doing it for the first time—remember the story itself, and the little pictures that I drew along the edge of the page. I was nine years old, a shy, odd, gangling child who found it hard to make friends and hated everything about school except for its library of books—especially A. A. Milne's classic, *Winnie the Pooh*. I loved that book so much that I can even remember the typeface and the clothbound hardcover. I remember, too, my class teacher reading it out loud when we had worked hard enough and deserved a treat. I loved that book so much that when she finished the last page I went home, bereft, and wrote a Pooh story of my own. I was enthralled by the characters of Winnie, Eeyore, Piglet, Kanga, Roo, and Tigger, and I wasn't prepared to let them go. They were my friends every bit as much as Christopher Robin's.

I thought the resulting story was mine too—mine alone—but things take on a life of their own when you write them down, as I was to find out! One afternoon, my class teacher picked up a tatty exercise book that looked strangely familiar, and said, "Today we're going to have a story by Pauline Fisk." I nearly died. She waved my book at me, an expression of triumph on her face as if she might have failed so far to "bring me out" but had got me now! I was ordered to leave my desk by the window, come up to the front of the class, and read my story out loud.

Even now I can remember standing there, trying to decide whether to grab the book and run. But I didn't—and I've been glad ever since! Instead I opened the book and started reading as fast as I could, lisping and stumbling through my metal-braced teeth and dying deaths because now everyone would know how really weird I was. The process seemed to take forever, however fast I tried to read, but finally I finished and silence fell over the class. I waited for the laughter to break out, scarcely daring to look at anyone. Then the clapping began. I looked up in a red haze of embarrassment, and a classful of children looked back as if they'd never seen me before. They had loved my story. They'd never known that I could write like that. Now they wanted me to do more.

My first commission! How can I ever forget it? That day I made a serious career decision to become a writer when I grew up. Suddenly everything about myself—all the oddities and contradictions—made sense. I didn't know it then, but I had stumbled upon the conflicting elements that make up a writer; the secret life with its need for privacy, but the exhibitionism too—wanting to be noticed and longing to communicate. All I knew for then was that I'd loved writing my story, turning it into words, and I'd also loved having an audience. Now I had a way of reaching people inside—of getting beyond their prejudices about who that strange, shy girl might be, sitting at the window desk, and enabling them to make friends with me.

They had caught a glimpse of who I really was. I had learned that through the means of story I could make connections.

From that time on, I never wanted to be anything else. I may have been only nine, with a sketchy understanding of what authors actually did, but like a baby bird who had found its wings I knew where I was going. This had its downside, of course—it's great to know what you want to be, but try replying "become an author" to the question "What are you going to do when you leave school?" and the very good question will come straight back at you: "Yes, but what are you actually going to do?"

In the meantime, my parents bought me a portable typewriter and I set about my apprenticeship. No longer did I care if people knew I had a secret life inside my head. I was writing stories as if my life depended on them, heading for the goal of publication, eager to join the world of books with my name on the spine. To this end I started sending short stories and poems off to magazines. They may have been childish offerings, but I was every bit as serious about them as any adult writer. Not that the magazines I targeted saw it like that! The rejection slips started rolling in and I soon discovered that the best way of handling disappointment is to start again on something new.

This I did, copying the styles of authors I admired and hoping this would make me sound like a "proper" writer. If I could only write like Dylan Thomas or Hans Christian Andersen, Ray Bradbury or Raymond Chandler, Emily Brontë or C. S. Lewis or Alan Garner, then perhaps one day someone would publish me.

So I struggled on, failing to realize that copying other writers' styles may be fine when you're nine, and even fine when you're an adolescent, but it's anything but when you reach twenty-three. This was my age when I had my first literary success—a collection of terrible short stories crafted in what I fondly imagined was J. R. R. Tolkien's lofty, epic tone—and written in a pseudonym that I will never divulge! I was so proud to be published at long last, and yet I realized that something was seriously wrong with my precious book. One reviewer said, "this author will win prizes one day," but another commended her child for throwing it down the toilet.

Obviously this hurt—but not half as much as it embarrassed me to read the book again some years later! But by this time I could see that the fault lay with the voice. It wasn't Tolkien's and it certainly wasn't mine—I had made sure of that, carefully editing out anything that sounded like me, as if afraid that my own voice would doom the work to failure.

And in the meantime I had given up on my writing career. Perhaps I'd lost my nerve. Perhaps the struggle to succeed had proved too much for me. Or perhaps fear of failure had got to me, and I stopped writing because I thought I couldn't do it well enough.

Whatever the reasons, I didn't write for years, and when I started again it was at the most unlikely time—after the birth of my fifth child. Suddenly, with little opportunity to do anything about it, the old longing rose up unbearably inside of me. What had happened to that girl who'd worked, and longed, and striven, and written, and hoped, and dreamed throughout her childhood years? I felt as if I'd lost the best of myself.

So I started writing again, making the opportunity by getting up at five each morning before the family awoke—and writing in my own voice this time, not someone else's. It was as if I had come full circle, returning to the child whose only voice was her own, and who knew that writing gave her power. And when the resulting novel, *Midnight Blue*, finally hit the bookshelves—and went on to win the Smarties Book Prize as best British children's novel of the year—its spine contained no pseudonym this time, but the name of a little girl who had dreamt big and lived in hope.

THE ARTS

Talent and persistence are two of the clues to
success in the arts. Here are the stories of those who
achieved fame as artists, actors, musicians,
and singers.

Introduction to

Ken Burns

I was passionately aware of history throughout my upbringing even though I never majored in history or had taken special history courses in school.

But Ken Burns knew in high school that filmmaking would be a great career—and he was determined to not only *do it*, but to become the winner of an Academy Award.

"I was so blessed," said Burns, "by knowing as a teenager just what I wanted to do." What has driven Burns to produce some of the most acclaimed documentary films for public television in the past twenty-five years began with the desire to make the past "come alive." "You wake the dead" is how one friend describes his films, such as the series on Louis Armstrong, Jackie Robinson, Abraham Lincoln, and Thomas Jefferson.

After graduating from Hampshire College in Amherst, Massachusetts, in 1975, Burns made his first professional film when he was twenty-eight, though he looked, he said, like a twelve-year-old. He still looks much younger than his years. The film, about the building of the Brooklyn Bridge in New York City, was nominated for an Academy Award, received an American Film Festival blue ribbon, and gave him a Guggenheim Fellowship. Thanks to the incredible success of his documentary on the Civil War, his career has taken off after many years of earning almost no income from his struggling new company. He has now established a reputation that assures him financial support from many sources.

I think I have the best job in the country. It educates all parts of me. It requires me to be a good writer, editor, businessman, and fund-raiser. It requires me to use all aspects of myself.

Ken Burns has received honors from all over the world for all of his documentaries, including sixteen honorary degrees from colleges and universities across the country. He is not only proud of his professional accomplishments but proud of and dedicated to his two teenage daughters and all young people eager to learn about the world they live in.

Ken Burns
Starting Out as a Filmmaker

I like to make films about things I don't know, for then my audience shares in the process of discovery. Let me share with you what I've learned.

I was born in Brooklyn, New York. My father was finishing his studies in anthropology at Columbia University, then left New York for France when I was three months old. He returned to work in Delaware; Newark, New Jersey; and then Ann Arbor, Michigan. From an early age I was aware that my mother was terminally ill. The knowledge that she was dying throughout my upbringing really changed the way I looked at the world. She died a few months before my twelfth birthday after a long, heroic struggle. After I became successful, a friend of mine said I was somehow trying to keep my mother alive by recording history, that I was "waking the dead." Suddenly, after years of making documentaries, I understood my innate, organic interest in history. My father struggled in his own way with this loss, and with his own professional and personal problems. For all intents and purposes, my younger brother and I were orphans. Part of my ambition and drive was in reaction to seeing my father unable to connect.

When I entered Hampshire College's filmmaking course after graduating high school, there was a class brimming with students, but by the time I graduated, only a handful had completed the course for a bachelor's degree. I hoped to become a Hollywood filmmaker then, but my teachers, Jerome Liebling and Elaine Mayes, changed my way of thinking. They reminded me that there was so much more drama in *what is* and *what was* than anything the human imagination could think of that I was completely turned around and decided to become a documentary filmmaker. I'd never taken a formal history course, except one on Russian history, but I was passionately aware of history during my upbringing.

At Hampshire our teachers encouraged us to find our own way—to have a self-initiated project. Professor Liebling, a fine professional photographer, encouraged us to do a film for a nonprofit client, so in 1974 I began a half-hour film on Old Sturbridge Village.

Inside my head, every bell was ringing! I almost immediately got my marching orders. There was a wonderful moment while editing that film that I'll remember the rest of my life. Professor Liebling had been a very caring teacher and friend. His influence and help went well beyond the classroom. There was a moment when I was showing him an early rough cut of the film and he suggested some changes. I disagreed with him. He insisted and I insisted back . . . and then he let go. I realized at this almost terrifying and glorious moment that I was on my own. I had been so completely influenced by him that I do not remember the person I was before I met Jerome Liebling. It was a wonderful moment but also a kind of free-fall, in that I was not only able, but obligated to go on with the rest of my life and find my own way.

When you become a documentary filmmaker you take a vow of poverty and anonymity. For many years I made a meager living doing camera work, then started a small company called Florentine Films. My wife and I starved. We'd get a job once a month, getting just enough to pay the rent and nothing else. We were living in Amherst, Massachusetts, but worked as far away as New York City and Boston—and wouldn't charge for our hotel costs or a *per diem*, which made us attractive to clients but it didn't pay us enough to live on.

I started my first independent film, about the Brooklyn Bridge, when I was twenty-three years old. I raised some money from foundations and corporations, enough to start shooting in '79. It took more than two years to complete. We struggled for years and years. Some years I earned only $2,500, or nothing, having used all the grant money to pay expenses first. The real payback has been that the success of these films generated a new interest in American history.

I'm often asked where my ideas come from. Some think of documentaries as bland, like castor oil. My response is that I'm asking the quintessential questions about Americans. Who are they? Where did they come from? Who are these complicated people who created America? Each answer is different. It might be about the Shakers, or demagogues, or the Civil War, or baseball. Some suggestions by people lodge in my head for twenty years and I don't do them. Then suddenly they nag at me . . . then one of them pops out. In general a film takes two and a half years to make. The series on jazz took almost seven years. In my films it's not just illustrating in images and words, but *some* combination that makes one plus one equal three.

Introduction to
Sidney Poitier

I remember—I was about twelve. I told my sister that I would like to go to Hollywood and become a cowboy.

I had seen my first movie—it was a cowboy movie, of course, and I thought it was the most amazing thing. I had no idea that Hollywood meant the movie business. I thought Hollywood was where they raised cows, and where they used horses to keep cows corralled . . . and I wanted to do that kind of work.

Movie star Sidney Poitier, of French and African ancestry, was born and raised on Cat Island in the Bahamas, an island only forty-six miles long and three miles wide with no paved road and a small population, almost all of whom were related to each other.

Poitier's father was a farmer who grew tomatoes, and his mother raised the family in a tiny house with no electricity, no running water, and no indoor plumbing. Having no money, their mother made all the children's clothes from grain sacks.

Despite all this, their lives were happy—with a beautiful beach, flowers, and fruit trees close by. It was a peaceful setting, untroubled by noisy traffic or crowds.

At fifteen Poitier entered the modern world when he went to live with an older brother in Miami, Florida. "As an immigrant teenager, I was still a kid, and I was still thinking like a kid, but I had something inside that was looking out for me."

Later Poitier moved to Harlem in New York City, tried out in The American Negro Theater, and then was offered a part in a movie in Hollywood. Only then did he begin to take acting seriously. When Poitier's first film *No Way Out*, was released, his family gathered in a theater on Nassau Island.

This was in 1950, and it was the first time my parents had ever seen a movie. My mother and father were sitting there, not knowing anything about movies. . . . Near the end of the movie Richard Widmark pistolwhips me. He's hitting me with this pistol—and my mother jumps up in the theater and yells, "Hit him back, Sidney! Hit him back! You never did nothing to him." That was my mother.

Sidney Poitier was the first black actor to receive an Academy Award, for his performance in the movie *Lilies of the Field* in 1963. After numerous starring roles in cinema, Poitier was selected as a recipient of the Screen Actors Guild's highest honor, a Lifetime Achievement Award. And at the Academy Awards in 2002, Poitier received an honorary Oscar for a lifetime of achievement.

Sidney Poitier

from The Measure of a Man

In Nassau, while learning about myself, I had become conscious of being pigeonholed by others, and I had determined then to always aim myself toward a slot of *my* choosing. There were too many images of what I could be. Where I could go. Too many images of wonderful, accomplished, interesting black people around and about for me to feel bad about my color.

In Miami, this strange new society started coming at me with point-blank force to hammer home its long-established, non-negotiable position on the color of skin, which declared me unworthy of human consideration, then ordered me to embrace the notion of my unworthiness. My reply was, "Who, me? Are you crazy? *Me?* You're talking to me?"

I was saying, "Hey, not only am I *not* that which you would make me. Here's what I in fact *am*. First of all, I'm the son of a really terrific guy, Reginald James Poitier. And Evelyn Poitier, my mom, who's a terrific woman. I have no evil designs: I'm a well-intentioned, meaningful person. I'm young, and I'm not particularly headstrong—though I can get pretty pissed. I'm a good person, and nothing you say can undo that. You can harp on that color crap as much as you want, but because of the way I was raised, I don't have a receptor that's gonna take in any of that."

Of course, over time, osmosis brings a lot of that sewage to you, and some of it does seep in, you know? But having arrived in America with a foundation that had had time to set, the Jim Crow way of life had trouble overwhelming me.

Vanity, which the dictionary says is an excess of pride, was the only way I could brace myself against the onslaught of the culture's merciless indictment of me. With no other means at my disposal to fight off society's intent to restrict my range of motion, to smother and suffocate me, excess was engaged to speak on my behalf. I was saying, "Okay, listen, you think I'm so inconsequential? Then try *this* on for size. All those who see unworthiness when they look at me and are given thereby to denying me value—to you I say, 'I'm not talking about being *as good as* you. I hereby declare myself *better* than you.'"

Miami shared a climate and lifestyle with the Caribbean, but its culture and mores were of the American South, 1940s Jim Crow–style, and nothing had prepared me to surrender my pride and self-regard sufficiently to accept those humiliations. In fact, it was quite the opposite. My values and my sense of self were already fully constructed.

Which is another way of saying that I was already a kid who wasn't gonna take any bullshit—from anybody.

While I was in no position to force society to accept me as I wanted to be accepted, I still had to let people know what *my* rules were. For a while I had a job as a delivery boy, and on one of my first assignments I was sent to a wealthy home in Miami Beach. I went to the front door and rang the bell, and a lady came to the door and said, "What do you want?"

"Good afternoon, ma'am," I said. "I've come to deliver your package from the drugstore."

"Get around to the back door where you belong," she snapped.

"But I'm *here*. Here's the package you ordered." I extended the bag containing her items.

She huffed and slammed the door in my face. I just couldn't understand what her problem was. I set the package down on the step in front of the door and left. I didn't think any more about it.

A couple of nights later, when I came home my brother's house was completely dark, and the family was lying on the floor, huddled together as if they were in a state of siege. It seems the Klan had been there looking for me, and everyone in the house was terrified. Everyone except me. Being new and from a different culture, I was wide-eyed with *curiosity*, mostly at the family's reaction. I just couldn't get used to this strange place and this strange way of behaving.

Later, I would carry that theme, detached from questions of

color and race, all the way into the theater world, where it would become a personal standard, applicable to creative excellence and professional competitiveness. Marlon Brando was an idol of mine, a consummate artist and one of the good guys. I aimed to be *better* than even him.

But I didn't need anyone to torture me or deny me or coddle me or cajole me into having that kind of drive. I was born with an innate curiosity and it took me to the damnedest places.

When I was small the world was an Eden. I woke up in the morning saying, 'I'm seven and I'm free! I can walk to the ocean and I can jump in. My brothers kick my ass now and then, but that's okay. There's all this newness! There's life! There's girls! There's that damned ditch that nearly got me killed. It's a whole world of fascinating challenges.'

Natural threats laid the foundation, but there was always a who or a what or a condition challenging me to prove my value. Pushing, forcing, threatening me to be better. Always better. I was challenged to understand all the abuse in the world. When I got to Nassau, it was race and class and economics, a colonial system that was very hostile. So my motto was *Never leave home without a fixed commitment.* I couldn't deal with those awesome odds either by waiting for society to someday have a change of heart or by saying, "I'm gonna be as good, one day, as you are." My heart said, "I'm already as good. In fact, I'm starting out with better material, and I am going to be better." How do you like *them* apples?

Young blacks coming up in America were frequently

subjected to parental lectures, almost all of which carried the same message: "Face this reality. You're gonna have to be twice as good as the white folks in order to get half as much." That was drilled into them. Bahamian lectures had another ring. "Get that education. Get out there and work. Get out there and hustle. Take whatever opportunities there are, and use them as stepping-stones."

There was simply no slot for a kid like me in a place like Florida, so I was itching to go north, despite the fact that I had no idea just how big the country was. As a teenager who tended to run away, I had made it as far as Tampa a couple of times . . .

Then a summer kitchen job in the mountains of Georgia put me within striking distance of breaking out . . . and at the end of the summer I found myself in the Atlanta bus station with thirty-nine dollars in my pocket. So I had to decide where I was going to go and what I was going to do.

[Poitier bought a one-way ticket to New York City and headed for Harlem.]

By the time I was eighteen years old, I was on the street in New York, struggling once again to survive on a dishwasher's pay.

If I could have pulled together the scratch, I would have headed back to Nassau—that's how big and fierce the prospect of another winter loomed over me. I even wrote directly to President Roosevelt for a loan, hitting him up for the hundred dollars I figured it would take. If I had succeeded in that effort, I probably would have spent my life at some low-level job taking care of tourists, spending Sundays sitting on a rock outside Nassau town trying to catch me a big fish. So even in my lack of luck, once again I was very lucky.

One day shortly after my discharge, as I was scanning the want ads for dishwasher openings, an article on the theatrical page of the *Amsterdam News*, a New York paper, caught my attention. I was between jobs and my pockets were nearly empty—so empty, in fact, that if no dishwashing position was available, I was ready to glom on to any kind of work that a black kid with no education might qualify for.

The page of want ad boxes faced the theatrical page, on which sat an article with a heading that read ACTORS WANTED. The gist of the article was that a theater group called The American Negro Theatre was in need of actors for its next production. My mind got to spinning. My eyes bounced back and forth between the want ad page and the theatrical page.

"What the hell," I thought. "I've tried dishwashers wanted, porters wanted, janitors wanted—why not try actors wanted?" I figured that I could do the work. Acting didn't sound any more difficult than washing dishes or parking cars. And the article didn't say the job required any particular kind of training. But when I went in and was auditioned on the spot, the man in charge quickly let me know—and in no uncertain terms—that I was misguided in my assumptions. I had no training in acting. I could barely read! And to top it off, I had a thick, singsong Bahamian accent.

He snatched the script from my hands, spun me around, grabbed me by the scruff of my neck and the back of my pants, and marched me on my tippytoes toward the door. He was seething. "You just get out of here and stop wasting people's time. Go get a job you can handle," he barked. And just as he threw me out, he ended with, "Get yourself a job as a dishwasher or something."

I have to tell you that his comments stung worse than any wasp on any sapodilla tree back in my childhood. His assessment was like a death sentence for my soul. I had never mentioned to him that I was a dishwasher. How did he know? If he *didn't* know, what was it about me that implied to this stranger that dishwashing would accurately sum up my whole life's worth?

Whatever it was, I knew I had to change it, or life was going to be mighty grim. There's something inside me—pride, ego, sense of self—that hates to fail at anything. I could never accept such a verdict of failure before I'd even begun my life! So I set out on a course of self-improvement. I worked nights, and on my evening meal-breaks I sat in a quiet area of the restaurant where I was employed, near the entrance to the kitchen, reading newspapers, trying to sound out each syllable of each unfamiliar word. An old Jewish waiter, noticing my efforts, took pity and offered to help. He became my tutor, as well as my guardian angel of the moment. Each night we sat in the same booth in that quiet area of the restaurant and he helped me learn to read.

My immediate objective was to prove that I could be an actor. Not that I had any real desire to go on the stage, mind you. Not that I had ever given acting a thought before reading that ad. I simply needed to prove to that man at the American Negro Theatre that Sidney Poitier had a hell of a lot more to him than washing dishes.

And it worked. The second time around they let me in. But it was still no slam dunk. In fact, I made the cut only because there were so few guys and they needed some male bodies to fill the new acting class. But soon after that first hurdle went down, another went up: because of my lack of education and experience, after a couple of months I was flunking out. And once again I felt that vulnerability, as if I'd fallen overboard into deep water. If I lost my chance at the theater, where would I be? One more black kid who could barely read, washing dishes on the island of Manhattan. So I worked out a deal. I became their janitor, and they let me continue to study.

Things began to improve, and maybe even *I* began to improve—as an actor, that is. But when it was time to cast the first big production, in walked this new guy, another kid from the Caribbean with whom the director had worked before. After all my studies, busting my ass trying to learn to act (not to mention busting my ass sweeping the walk and stoking the furnace), she was going to cast *him* in the lead. Well, I had to admit he was a pretty good-looking kid, and he had a nice voice. He could even sing a little.

I tried to find some consolation in the fact that they made

me the understudy, but little did I know. On the night of the first major run-through, the one night a significant casting director was coming to watch the show, the other Caribbean kid they'd cast for the lead—a kid named *Harry Belafonte*—couldn't make it. I had to go on for him, and son of a gun, the casting director liked what I did and called me.

"I'm preparing a version of *Lysistrata* for Broadway. Would you be available?"

Are you kidding?

Next thing I knew I was staring out into a sea of white faces from a Broadway stage, scared shitless as I fumbled for my lines as Polydorus.

The word *bad* cannot begin to accommodate my wretchedness. I mean, I was BAD. The stage fright had me so tightly in its grip that I was giving the wrong cues and jumbling the lines, and within a few moments the audience was rolling in the aisles.

The moment the curtain came down it was time for this Caribbean kid to run for cover. My career was over before it had begun, and the void was opening up once again to receive me. I didn't even go to the cast party, which meant that I wasn't around when the first reviews appeared.

The critics trashed the show. I mean, they *hated* it. But they liked me. I was so god-awful they thought I was good. They said they admired my "fresh, comedic gift."

If you saw this scenario in an old black-and-white movie on TV, would you believe it? I saw it in real life, and I certainly didn't. In my world, effort and reward were expected to settle into a natural balance. By any reasonable measure, I knew that I'd fallen short that evening. That was *my* critical assessment. That assessment, taken at its worth, created a big fat contradiction inside me. Maybe I just wasn't up to this acting thing. Maybe the man at the little theater in Harlem was right. Maybe I *should* "go out and get a job I could handle."

I couldn't shake the sense that failure was lurking somewhere in the wings, waiting to pick my bones if my doubts should become reality. Still, in the face of all that, I had to stay in charge of my life no matter how it all played out. Regardless of whatever (or whoever) else might have been looking out for me, I needed to know, first and foremost, that *I* was looking out for *myself.* Even when the dread of being shot down by failure twisted my insides into knots.

Did I misjudge this new culture? Should all the glitter that now seemed only inches beyond my reach have been taken with a grain of salt? Maybe natural balances weren't that easily found amid so much concrete and steel, amid so many machines pushing automobiles, lifting elevators, pulling trains. Or maybe, at the very bottom, I wasn't yet ready to accept that environment compromises values far more than values do their number on environment.

The play ran only four days. But to my surprise, my "triumph" in *Lysistrata* led immediately to another acting job as an understudy in a road show of *Anna Lucasta*, a job that lasted intermittently for several weeks.

Introduction to

Claire Bloom

I begged my mother for another chance to go to the theater, but there was no money.

When the Second World War began, the battles between Claire Bloom's parents escalated. Eddie, her irresponsible father, moved his family from house to house after each "get rich quick" venture failed. Leaving Eddie behind, Claire, her brother, and her mother left London for the United States, hoping that Claire's developing acting talent would help them find some financial and emotional security.

As a young teenager Claire's passion for acting gave her an emotional escape into a world of fantasy and a practical way of helping support her mother and brother during the war years.

Returning to Britain, Bloom's acting career blossomed. She starred in roles on stage in Ibsen's "A Doll's House," Tennessee Williams's "A Streetcar Named Desire," and O'Neill's "Long Day's Journey into Night." Her role at age nineteen in the movie "Limelight" with Charles Chaplin was the start of a successful film career.

Bloom also regularly performed in plays for television, both in the United States and Britain.

Claire Bloom

from *Leaving a Doll's House*

For my twelfth birthday present, Mother purchased tickets for both of us to attend a performance of a play on Broadway, entitled "Junior Miss." It left me longing for more. On one never-to-be-forgotten matinee day, we went to see Chekhov's "The Three Sisters." The leading players were Katharine Cornell, Ruth Gordon, Gertrude Musgrove, and Judith Anderson.

I recognized for the first time, as part of my barely formed sexual identity, the sisters' compulsion to replace their lost father with another masculine figure: a need so fundamental that Masha is drawn to an unattainable married man, Olga marries a pedantic schoolmaster many years her senior, and Irina is induced to become engaged to someone she doesn't love. All the more heartbreaking is that, at the close and despite their choices, there they are, still clinging to expectations of a better life.

From that moment on, my single desire was to act in a play by a great master. "The Three Sisters" was the genuine article.

I begged my mother for another chance to go to the theater, but there was no money. Mother adored the theater as much as I did, and promised me that when we returned home to England and things got better, we could go as often as we wished.

At about this time, I started to listen to a children's show on the radio: Robert Emory's "Rainbow Hour," a program of plays for children performed by child actors. An announcement was made inviting children wanting to take part in one of the broadcasts to write in, explaining why they wanted to act. With Mother's help, I composed a letter, which I sent eagerly and immediately; soon after, I received the reply, inviting me to an audition a few weeks later. Mother and I set off for the studio. Led into a brightly lit room, I was invited by a remote voice emanating from another studio to tell them about myself.

Mysteriously, the shy girl vanished and the confident performer took over. I went into every detail of my young life at extreme length until, in midlecture, I was suddenly interrupted and asked to read from a script. With almost superhuman self-assurance, I read the role of England's Queen Elizabeth I. I read the part in a blustery, rather bullying tone that I thought suitable to convey the character of a great queen. I was told to wait in the adjoining room while my attributes were discussed in private. After about half an hour, during which my entire future was seemingly suspended in midair, I met Mr. Emory himself, and was offered the role of Elizabeth I.

We went to celebrate the birth of my brilliant career as a "real actress" at the Automat on West 57th Street across from Steinway Hall.

To anyone who missed the wonders of the Horn and Hardart Automat, I can bear witness to its peculiar enchantment. The walls of the vast eating area were lined with metal containers bearing glass windows, in which rested every imaginable food available. The Automat was fast food with an element of fantasy, and, as a means of dining out, it was enchanting to a child—indeed, to many adults as well: it became the weekly treat for our family during our time in New York, a never-failing source of pleasure.

I arrived at the radio station the following week for the broadcast and made no major mistakes. Convinced that the entire world was listening to my radio debut, I was soon disabused. Apart from the Jorgensons and Cousin Lily, nobody's life appeared to have been changed in any way by my voice on the air.

That year I was cast as Gretel in Englebert Humperdinck's opera *Hansel and Gretel.* I had reached my full height and was a foot taller than the poor youth who sang Hansel. Although I was not then—nor was ever to become, alas—a good singer, I enjoyed every moment on stage, and was quite capable of carrying a tune. This time Mother was able to come and I had the thrill of showing her how much I had learned.

Introduction to
Clyde Bernhardt

In his autobiography, titled *I Remember: Eighty Years of Black Entertainment, Big Bands, and the Blues*, jazz trombonist Clyde Bernhardt remembers playing a "kazoo," a small, metal, handheld toy instrument. Being dirt poor, it was the only thing he could afford. This didn't stop Bernhardt from wanting to be a musician, however.

So, on November 1, 1919, at the age of fourteen, I packed my suitcase, left home, and went back to Badin. I was on my own. Papa would watch over me, I was sure. Everybody said I was independent like him. And kind of hard-headed and stubborn like Mama. They were right.

Somehow he was going to find the twenty-five dollars to buy his first trombone. It wasn't long before he became one of the most popular jazz trombonists of his day, performing with the best jazz and blues bands in the country.

Clyde Bernhardt

from I Remember: Eighty Years of Black Entertainment, Big Bands, and the Blues

I found living in our new working-class neighborhood strange. All the houses stuck together in a row. People coming in and going out all day, and night too. Whites. Blacks. Polish. Italians. Romanians.

Mama got a job in a beer factory, but when the smell got bad, took another as a domestic for a rich white lady. I tried hard, but jobs were scarce for little black boys.

By late October we moved three miles down to Steelton, Pennsylvania. This was a worse job-town for me than Harrisburg. Bethlehem had one of their biggest steel mills there, but I was too young to be hired. Mama was pushing me to find a job. I tried hard, I really did. Got up before daybreak and was at the food stores by 5:30, hoping to find something.

"What you doin' out here?" the man say.

"Looking for a job, sir. Need a good boy to help around?"

"Yeah, I do, but don't want no coloreds. Be on your way."

Mama said I wasn't trying hard enough. "You gettin' lazy like the rest of these Northern boys," she mumbled.

I been secretly writing to Mr. Kaufman in Badin, and he kept answering, saying my Alcoa job was still open.

So, on November 1, 1919, at the age of fourteen, I packed my suitcase, left home, and went back to Badin. I was on my own. Papa would watch over me, I was sure. Everybody said I was independent like him. And kind of hard-headed and stubborn like Mama. They were right.

The day I returned to Badin, Mr. Kaufman put me up in his house and started me again at the Alcoa plant. A few weeks later, I met Mr. Charlie Crowell, the same Mr. Crowell that made my shoeshine box when I was helping out my sick papa. Now he was the railroad station agent of the Western Union telegraph office in Badin and was looking for a new messenger boy. Offered me the job.

Everybody knew they never had no colored Western Union messenger in that town before. Or any town in North Carolina that I heard of. When he explained the twenty-five-dollar monthly pay I get, plus the daily tips, special fees for far deliveries, free telegrams to Mama, free train fare all over the United States, one week paid vacation, and four weeks paid sick or emergency time off. I grabbed it. It was the best job I ever had. But I told Mr. Kaufman to hold my Alcoa job open, just in case.

I worked from 9 A.M. to 6:30 P.M. and went to school five nights a week. They gave me a little cap with the words

"Western Union" printed on it, a special blue jacket, blank telegram pads, and a indelible pencil. Taught me to bow correctly and explained good front-door manners: Yes sir. No sir. Thank you. Good day.

I sent Mama twenty dollars a month and put everything else I made in a good U.S. Postal Savings account. That was the safest bank in the country.

They never saw a readier boy than me. I hustled, yes I did. If a message come in, I always seemed to be standing next to Mr. Crowell ready to go. If it was past 6:30, after everybody left, they knew I still was there to take it out. No extra pay, but I was ready to go. Many of the older customers couldn't read or write, so I help with that too, compose their messages, told them how to save money by keeping within ten words. Always talked polite to everyone, especially when they start crying when I knock on their door, because many telegrams were death notices.

By the end of the month I was delivering more than all the white boys and making double their tips.

Wasn't long before I bought my own bicycle, the only messenger boy to have his own wheel, as we called it. Then I was able to take telegrams some five miles up the highway, and way off in the woods. The only thing I didn't like was them slippery snakes, all wiggling and skittering across the road. Then I get off my wheel, find a big stick, and beat them old snakes to a low gravy. I hated them.

Shows such as "Oh Baby" and "Oh Daddy" with pretty

white chorus girls and singers barnstormed through town at the Badin Theater. I was always backstage taking it all in.

I never did go back to the Alcoa job. Worked for Western Union till April 1, 1921, when I got homesick for my family and returned to Steelton.

Mama wrote me to come back, and from that time on, she treated me as a adult. Gave me the understanding a son should get. No more whippings, no more meanness. I guess I earned her respect.

After I turned sixteen in 1921, I wasn't required to complete my schooling. Moving around so much caught me in the middle of the eighth grade when I stopped.

I remember it was the first part of October 1921. The great Ethel Waters was making a personal appearance with her Black Swan Troubadours at the Chestnut Street Auditorium. Fletcher Henderson was directing a seven-piece band and Joe Smith was on trumpet. When I got there the man wouldn't let me in, said I had to be sixteen. But I *was* sixteen, only didn't look it.

As I was standing on the curb, this man came over, told me if I helped him sell soda pop at the show, we both get in free. Even gave me fifty cents. Yes sir. Papa was watching over me that night.

It was a great show, and when Joe Smith started playing the first solo chorus of "Bugle Blues" from the top balcony, every nerve in my body started jumping. Ethel Waters sang her "At the New Jump Steady Ball" and "Down Home Blues."

After they got to know me at the door, I was there regular.

I seen every show that came to town and then run home and try to imitate the music on my kazoo. We called them "cazoots" then. Sometimes I get to fooling around with my friends, make believe we all hot jazz musicians. One fellow had a cazoot saxophone, another had one in the shape of a trumpet, someone else had a toy accordion with keys painted on—only made one note if he opened and closed it. I tied a comb wrapped in paper on a old broomstick and made believe I had a slide trombone.

One day I was passing Nathan's Pawnshop in Blackberry Alley and spotted this pretty silver-plated trombone hanging in the window. It was well worn and beat up a little, but it sure looked nice to me. And the sign read "Only $25." When I brought it home, Mama asked what I was planning to do with it.

"Learn to play," I said firmly. Didn't even know how to put the damn thing together because there was no instructions, but I sat and looked at that slide horn for hours. Even patted it a couple times.

Everybody talked about Mr. Joe Vennie, the best black music teacher in Harrisburg. Said he was strict, didn't take anybody he couldn't teach or wasn't capable. But I knew his daughter Tillie was one of the best local piano players and worked dances around town with her own band.

It was 7 P.M., Monday night, May 8, 1922, when I showed up at his front door holding my horn just like a regular musician. A stern-looking old man answered my knock.

"My name is Clyde Bernhardt," I said faintly, standing there scared to death. "Can you teach me trombone?"

"Come in, son," he said and led me in the parlor.

"I got my own horn here, Mr. Vennie," I blurted out, "and I wanna learn to play it."

"Let me see what you got there, boy," and he opened the case, took out the parts, and looked them over like he was inspecting a new horse. Before I knew it, he put them all together and was moving the slide in and out.

"Very slow," he mumbled, "and it's a mightly old instrument. But we can try."

"How much you gonna charge me, Mr. Vennie?"

"*If* I decide to teach you, it will be fifty cents a lesson. And a lesson is exactly one-half hour. No more, no less."

"Can we start right now, Mr. Vennie?"

"You jumping on something hard, boy."

I knew that. I was sure I could learn if somebody only give me a chance. He started explaining all the parts to me, showed the seven positions, and blew a note in each.

Handing me the horn, he put my hands on correctly, then told me to blow just as he did. I took a deep breath and let out a mighty blow. My cheeks poked out and my eyes bugged. The wind rushed through the horn, and I felt proud I made such a big blow. Unfortunately, no sound came out!

Introduction to

Pablo Casals

I see no particular merit in the fact that I was an artist at the age of eleven. I was born with an ability, with music in me, that is all. No special credit was due me. The only credit we can claim is for the use we make of the talent we are given.

For Pablo Casals, the famous Spanish musician/composer, the door to a bright future was the early discovery of his musical talent, a door that almost shut tight when he reached early adolescence.

From the time he was four, Pablo had a remarkable sense of pitch and could name each note on the piano. Although his father, an underpaid church organist, recognized his son's talent and love of music, he did not want Pablo to live the same meager life of a musician as he did. The struggle finally came to a head when Pablo turned eleven. It became clear that he needed to go to Barcelona to find more professional training than his village of Vendrell could offer . . . or give up the notion of making music his career.

My father was astonished. "What in the world are you talking about? How can Pablo possibly go to Barcelona? We simply do not have the money."

"We will find a way," my mother replied. "Pablo is a musician. This is what he was made to be. He must go anywhere necessary. There is no other choice."

His mother prevailed and Pablo was sent to the Municipal School of Music in Barcelona to study the cello. When, years later, Casals became a world-renowned performer, his mother, he said, was not particularly impressed. She had expected it.

Casals went into voluntary exile from his beloved Spain to protest the rule of dictator Francisco Franco after the Spanish Civil War, raising money for Spanish Refugee Aid through his concerts.

The only weapons I ever had are my cello and conductor's baton. And during the Spanish Civil War I used them as best I could to support the cause in which I believed . . . the cause of freedom and democracy.

For almost seventy years Casals performed throughout Europe and North and South America.

Pablo Casals
from Joys and Sorrows

When I was eleven years old, I heard the cello played for the first time. That was the beginning of a long and cherished companionship! A trio had come to play at a concert in Vendrell—a pianist, a violinist, and a cellist. My father took me to the concert. It was held at the small hall of the Catholic Center, with an audience of townspeople, fishermen, and peasants, who, as always for such an occasion, were dressed in their Sunday clothes. The cellist was Josep García, a teacher at the Municipal School of Music in Barcelona; he was a handsome man with a high forehead and a handlebar mustache; and his figure somehow seemed fitted to his instrument. When I saw his cello I was fascinated by it—I had never seen one before. From the moment I heard the first notes I was overwhelmed. I felt as if I could not breathe. There was something so tender, beautiful, and human—yes, so very human—about the sound. I had never heard such a beautiful sound before. A radiance filled me. When the first composition was ended, I told my father, "Father, that is the most wonderful instrument I have ever heard. That is what I want to play."

After the concert I kept talking to my father about the cello, pleading with him to get me one. From that time, more than eighty years ago, I was wedded to the instrument. It would be my companion and friend for the rest of my life. I had, of course, found joy in the violin, the piano, and other instruments, but for me the cello was something special and unique. I began playing my violin holding it like a cello.

My mother understood what had happened. She told my father, "Pablo shows such enthusiasm for the cello that he must have the chance really to study it. There is no teacher here in Vendrell who is qualified to teach him properly. We must arrange for him to go to the School of Music in Barcelona."

My father was astonished. "What in the world are you talking about?" he asked. "How can Pablo possibly go to Barcelona? We simply do not have the money."

My mother said, "We will find a way. I will take him there. Pablo is a musician. This is his nature. This is what he was made to be. He must go anywhere necessary. There is no other choice."

My father was not at all convinced—he was, in fact, already thinking about my following the trade of a carpenter in order to earn a living. "You have delusions of grandeur," he told my mother.

Their discussions on the subject became more and more frequent and intense. It troubled me greatly. I felt I was to blame for the disagreement between them. I asked myself how I could end it, but I didn't know what to do. Finally, my father reluctantly gave in. He wrote a letter to the Municipal School of Music in Barcelona asking if they would accept me as a pupil. He also said that I would need a small cello, three-quarter size, and asked if they knew an instrument maker who could make one for me.

Even so, after the school had responded favorably and as the time approached for my going to Barcelona, my father continued to express misgivings.

"Dear Carlos," my mother would tell him, "you may be sure that this is right. This is what has to be. It is the only thing for Pablo."

My father would shake his head. "I do not understand, I do not understand."

And she would say, "I know that, but you must have faith. You must be confident; you must."

It was a truly remarkable thing. My mother had had some musical training, but she was not of course a musician in the sense my father was. Yet she knew what my future was to be. She had known, I believe, from the beginning; it was as if she had some special sensitivity, a peculiar prescience. She knew; and she always acted on the knowledge with a firmness and certainty and calmness that has never ceased to amaze me. This was so not only about my studying in Barcelona, but in later years, on other occasions when I was at a crossroads in my career. It was so also with my younger brothers, Luis and Enrique; when they were still children, she knew the paths that they would follow. And later when I was playing concerts in many parts of the world and some success had come to me, she was happy but I would not say impressed. She had assumed this would be so.

During my life I myself have come to understand what she believed. I have come to the feeling that what happens must happen. I do not mean of course that there is nothing we can do about what we are or what we shall become. Everything about us is in a constant state of change—that is the way of nature; and we ourselves are changing all the time, for we are part of nature. We have the duty always to work to change ourselves for the better. But I do believe we have our destinies.

Introduction to

Beverly Sills

When *I was fourteen, I had urged my mother to please tell Papa that I wanted to be an opera star and that he really ought to have a more positive attitude about it. "Listen, Morris," my mother said. "The child wants to be an opera star." He never looked up from his soup and replied, "The child will go to college and be smart."*

"No, Morris," said my mother. "The two boys will go to college and be smart. This one will be an opera singer."

Beverly Sills was born Belle Miriam Silverman, in Brooklyn, New York, in 1929. Her mother's passion for music, especially opera, seeped into her daughter's life like the heady sea air of Sea Gate, Brooklyn. By age seven, "Bubbles," as she was then called, had memorized twenty-two arias from a phonograph recording that her mother played day after day. Each Saturday they took a two-hour ride to Manhattan for Beverly's piano and voice lessons. Impressed by Beverly's talent, her teacher helped get her a spot on "Major Bowes' Amateur Hour," a radio program, and on a soap opera called "Our Girl Sunday." When she turned twelve, Beverly's parents decided it was time for her to lead a more normal existence and had her "retire." But that was not to be the end of *that* career.

After starring in many Gilbert and Sullivan operettas, Sills finally had her long-awaited debut with the New York City Opera and the Metropolitan Opera, becoming one of their leading singers. After more than thirty years on stage, she became director of New York's Lincoln Center for the Performing Arts, where she served for eight years before retiring in 2002.

Beverly Sills
from Bubbles: A Self-Portrait

In 1944, when I was fifteen, I decided to come out of retirement. I began reading theatrical publications for announcements of chorus auditions for Broadway musicals. You must understand that for a fifteen-year-old-girl who dreamed of being an opera star, the starting possibilities then were nil. The New York City Opera had not yet been established. There were fewer opera companies, than there are today, and no regional companies. [My teacher] Miss Liebling thought it was a good idea for me to begin auditioning around because it would give me opportunities to sing before live audiences. (I had sung before large numbers of people only a few times in my life—on "Major Bowes' Amateur Hour;" at an amateur contest in junior high school, where I won ten dollars and a policeman had to escort me and my enormous earnings home; at the première of my movie at the Savoy Theatre in Brooklyn when I was seven, attended by about half the

Metropolitan Life Insurance Company; and at Miss Liebling's dinner parties for twenty-five people.) But she did not like the idea of my auditioning for Broadway choruses; *no* self-respecting would-be opera star, she felt, should take a job as a chorus singer, much less in a chorus line.

Nevertheless, I went auditioning. I had turned into a tall, statuesque fifteen-year-old with very long blond hair. I must have looked like a show girl because I was offered every chorus job I ever auditioned for. I turned them all down. But at one chorus audition for a Broadway show that J. J. Shubert was producing—it was called *Love in the Snow*—I was offered the job of understudy to Anne Jeffreys, the star. When I raced home to break the news, my father, who was not aware that I had been auditioning, hit the ceiling. Out of the question, he said. I was going to get a college education first, and *then* if I wanted to go on stage, fine. But I was going to have a college degree in my pocket in case things didn't work out for me on the stage.

That was that. In our house, as in most Jewish middle-class households of the time, the father's word was law. And my father was a very positive man; every sentence he spoke had a period at the end. When I was about thirteen, for example, he said to me, "Listen, your mother doesn't smoke and she doesn't drink and you're not going to either and that's the end of the discussion." And it was. I never smoked and I still do not drink, except wine. There was never a question of my rebelling against my father's decision about the Shubert offer, or of running away from home. Besides, I loved my father.

Once more unto the breach, dear Miss Liebling. She knew J. J. Shubert well and arranged for me to have an audition with the great man himself. It was love at first sight. I guess that I was the baby girl J. J. had never had and perhaps he was the grandpa I had never had. We read scripts together, both of us playing all kinds of parts and he trying hard to get rid of my Brooklyn accent. He brought people in to teach me how to wear makeup. Frequently we would have dinner in his apartment and do jigsaw puzzles. Then I would subway back to Brooklyn, doing my homework on board, so that I would be home—as agreed—by nine o'clock.

I was enjoying myself tremendously—making new friends, exploring Greenwich Village (where the lifestyle then was considerably different from what it is now). I discovered the art film, mostly French, and was suddenly aware that there was a Europe on the other side of the ocean. Would I ever get to France, I dreamed, where everyone must look like Lily Pons?

I remember standing room at the Met, holding an armful of school books, wearing bobby socks and brown-and-white saddle shoes and a big Sloppy Joe sweater, listening to the opera and wanting it to go on forever. The war was on and we lived in terrible fear because both my brothers were in combat service. From Norton Point, the farthest tip of Sea Gate, we could see the ships being loaded with soldiers leaving for Europe and the wind would bring back the sounds of their voices—the saddest sound in the world.

It was a crazy-mixed-up time in my life—I was growing up. Musically it was an incredibly exhilarating period. What J. J. was cooking up for me was a Gilbert and Sullivan repertory tour that would enable me to sing roles in seven different operettas. But first there were my parents to convince. My father was dead against it—I was too young, he said, he didn't want my mother to travel with me, she belonged at his side, and so on. But J. J.—and my mother—finally won. Mama found a chaperone for me, a nice, religious girl in the cast. She was to room with me, see that my clothes were packed properly, that I made all the trains, was taken to the theater and brought straight home afterward. And off we went on tour. My chaperone was also supposed to do my hair, using a recipe my mother had invented to keep it a lovely golden color. The recipe called for two parts of gold bleach to one part of red rinse, plus peroxide. The chaperone got it backward—two parts red to one part gold. That's how I became a redhead. I liked it and I have remained a redhead ever since.

The only trouble with my chaperone was that she had a tendency to entertain her men friends in our room until the wee hours. When Mama learned of this, through a letter a chorus boy in the cast wrote her, she promptly fired the girl chaperone and appointed her informant my chaperone for the rest of the tour. (*That* chaperone later served a term in jail for murder. We corresponded all during his term and he sent me the most gorgeous needlepoint pillows he had made. A week after he was paroled, he died of a heart attack and my husband and I helped bury him.)

It was 1945 and I was sixteen. My salary was $100 a week—which seemed an enormous sum at the time—out of which my father insisted that I buy a twenty-five-dollar war bond. By that time I had transferred from Erasmus High School in Brooklyn to the Professional Children's School in Manhattan. While on tour I finished that school's curriculum via a correspondence course. My father couldn't bear the idea of my graduating with a correspondence-course diploma; to him it was a waste of my brain. He was even more upset when Frank Fay, who handed out the diplomas at graduation, patted me on the fanny as I went by and said, "Boy, they didn't make them like you when *I* was graduating!"

My father was very worried about my future. To show him that I was still his smart little baby girl, I won a mathematics scholarship to Fairleigh Dickinson College. He was overjoyed and kept urging me to take advantage of the scholarship. But I had other ideas. I had returned from the Gilbert and Sullivan tour with a fistful of marvelous reviews. I had learned a good deal about stagecraft. I had learned how to project my speaking voice on stage. (Although my accent has always remained New York, I did at least manage to get rid of a good bit of the Brooklyn tinge. You just don't perform Gilbert and Sullivan sounding as though you came from the Ebbetts Field bleachers.) I had worked very hard with my music, I was a very disciplined young girl, and my desire to perform in front of an audience had become insatiable. Fairleigh Dickinson? Not a chance. I was going to be an opera star—and a very serious one. Period.

SCIENCE, MEDICINE, AND INVENTION

Seeking answers is what science, medicine, and inventions are all about. It took Charles Darwin halfway around the world. Others searched weeks and months alone in their labs. Their answers sometimes change the way we live.

Introduction to
Mae Jemison

*O*ne thing I was consistent about was testing limits—mine and other people's . . . I would look around for an opportunity and find a potential way to get it done. I would figure out my best shot at accomplishing it, then go for it.

In her autobiography, titled *Find Where the Wind Goes*, astronaut Dr. Mae Jemison describes all the twists and turns of her growing up with two older siblings and caring parents. As a normal but unusually bright child who was afraid of the dark, afraid of heights, and teased by her older brothers, and who was a clumsy but enthusiastic dancer, she was also one of the only African-American students in her elementary school in Chicago's South Side.

After finishing high school with high marks in science and mathematics, she received a scholarship to Stanford University to study chemical engineering. At the same time she studied African-American culture and learned to speak Swahili.

Reversing direction, she then decided to become a physician and entered Cornell Medical School in New York City. After graduation she joined the Peace Corps and traveled the back roads of West Africa as one of the youngest medical officers to serve in this capacity.

Jemison recalls that at age ten, she had been fascinated with the television show *Star Trek*. "I already knew that I would travel in space," Jemison wrote in her autobiography. "I had an encyclopedia that gave the step by step details of how a human would arrive on the surface of the moon."

Her story of how she changed from the little girl afraid of heights to becoming the only woman astronaut on the spaceship *Endeavor* in 1987 is both extraordinary and inspiring.

"So many things happened since I left NASA, in 1993," wrote Jemison. After six years with NASA, having been the first woman of color to be sent into space, Jemison started a technology consulting firm and an international science camp for children. She also teaches environmental studies at Dartmouth College.

The recipient of numerous awards, she was inducted into the National Women's Hall of Fame in 1993.

Mae Jemison
from Find Where the Wind Goes

"No, I don't know what sickle cell anemia is."

"Then you need to look it up. You're always talking about space exploration. Why don't you think about something else?"

I hate it when she does that. Whenever my mother wants me to try something, she doesn't tell me what it is or what to do, she just drops it on the table like a loaf of bread and leaves. You can pick it up and eat it if you want or you can starve. Your choice. Not a lot of preamble, no warning, at least that I pay attention to. No real direction, and the older I get, the less direction and the more challenge, doubt of my abilities seems implicit in that casually dropped phrase or topic.

So there it was. Sickle cell anemia. Dropped on the metaphorical table. A challenge. She wasn't going to tell me. Since I think I'm so cool and science smart, a junior in high school, I should know. Phooey. She did this just because I said

I want to do a science project [for the science fair at school]. Just because I don't want to work anymore with the goldfish swimming in mazes after being exposed in varying concentrations of thyroxin. So what if the cats constantly went fishing in bowls of fish that were scattered throughout the breakfast room. I always cleaned up the goldfish flipping and lying gasping on the floor. I know it costs a lot to buy the goldfish. Okay, the project was a bit of a bummer—their little fish brains had a problem with mazes. But I did do a lot of research on pyridoxine and the effects of thyroid hormone; and I learned how to build a maze with epoxy and acrylic pieces.

Oh well, this year, sickle cell anemia. I just peeked. It's still just lying on that psychological table. No clues left behind. Why did she do that? I don't know. Maybe to make my work harder than the challenges school provided. I couldn't even gloat and say I knew what sickle cell anemia was.

So do some *research*. The dictionary says "sickle cell anemia is an inherited blood disease found primarily in people of African ancestry." Okey dokey. What do I do now?

At fifteen I was confident and believed that the world and people wanted to help. Or at least I could talk them into helping me. Who could I turn to for help with this? I knew that hematology was the study of blood diseases. I had once been to Cook County Hospital to visit my aunt, so why not call their lab?

"Just do it, Mae."

"All right, all right."

"I don't have the number."

"So call the operator." I often had these two-sided dialogues with myself.

"There, the phone is ringing. Are you happy? It's not even the hematology lab. It's the main hospital telephone."

"Ask for the hematology lab."

"And what do I say when hematology answers? I don't . . . Oh, hello. My name is Mae Jemison, I am a junior at Morgan Park High School and I'm working on a science project . . . Oh, okay. Yes, I would like to speak to the chief hematology lab technician."

"Slow your breathing down. Do not hyperventilate. Just say . . ."

"Yes, my name is Mae Jemison and I am working on a science project on sickle cell anemia . . . Uh huh. High school chemistry and biology. Yes, I read a lot and am good at lab work."

"Yes, I have done science projects before. I would like to help."

"Yes, I can come . . . Next Tuesday at 4:30 P.M. Sure."

"Mother, how do you get to Cook County Hospital?"

I was a little nervous. I had never taken the train and bus alone all the way from the south side of Chicago to the west side, where Cook County Hospital Hektoen Hematology Labs were located over on Rush Street. In fact, to my recollection I had never traveled to the west side by train with or without anyone; we always drove over. By the time I took the 112th Street bus from in front of Morgan Park High School to the Dan Ryan Train Station at 95th and State Streets, then transferred to the el train and arrived at Rush Street, it was almost 4:30 P.M.

I met the technician on the eighth-floor lab, slightly breathless, but profoundly impressed with myself for getting there on time. The technician, a middle-aged African-American man, asked me what I knew about sickle cell and chemistry. At that point I knew sickle cell disease could be fatal by the time a person became a teenager and historically, very few people survived into their twenties with the disease. I also knew that children and people who had it were often ill, got infections, did not grow well, and had episodes of severe pain called "crises" in their joints and internal organs. I knew that the illness got its name because the red blood cells of people who suffered with it at times were shaped like sickles or quarter moons instead of circles like normal red blood cells. But I did not know how it was diagnosed or treated. As I sat there this wonderful man told me how they diagnosed sickle cell anemia in the lab. He showed me equipment, quizzed me on pH and making solutions: molar, normal, and volumetric. I did know some chemistry. I could tell he was impressed. He told me I should come in twice a week.

Over the next month, the technician taught me how to recognize the difference between the electrophoretic movement (how molecules move under the influence of electricity) of normal or A hemoglobin, sickle cell or S hemoglobin, fetal or F hemoglobin, and what the pattern looked like that indicated a person had sickle cell anemia, sickle cell trait, normal hemoglobin, thalassemia, or sickle-cell and thalassemia combined. (Hey, I know the words are big. But I had to look them up, so you should give it a try, too.) I made solutions for the entire laboratory and set up the electrophoresis chambers. I also learned to do the preliminary test to see if it was even necessary to test the blood sample for hemoglobinopathies. (That's abnormal hemoglobin for those of you not in the know. Now that I was learning how to use these big words I was *très* cool.) The lab tech was very impressed with how quickly I learned. So was I—within a month I had the jargon and the swagger.

Then one day, while standing next to the centrifuge, waiting for it to spin down so I could remove a sample, I looked up and there was this white, fortyish, male doctor looking at me. In fact, he was standing over me waiting for me to turn around.

I casually took my samples out of the centrifuge and said hello. He introduced himself as the head of the hematology department. He had a German/Swedish-sounding accent. I couldn't distinguish any further, though I could recognize French, Spanish, British, Southern, East Indian, and nasal Midwestern twang. He politely inquired who I was and what I was doing in the lab.

Not being overly timid, I answered with my name and politely stated that I was working on a project on sickle cell anemia. I don't recall if he smiled or not, but the next words are imprinted on my memory. He asked quite simply, "What is your hypothesis?"

For the second time in this particular science project adventure, someone, not even my mother this time, had me at a loss for words. After moving my mouth and trying to find an answer, I said I was doing a demonstration project. I knew how to do all this lab work. The doctor replied, "No. If you are going to work in my lab on a science project, you will have to get a hypothesis, do more background research and experimentation." He relieved me of my samples, gave them to one of the lab techs, and took me to his office. We discussed a bit more of my background and what a science experiment entailed. Of course I knew about hypotheses and the experimental method. I just didn't have one. He gave me assignments to look up a couple of authors and scientific papers, and to contact the National Institutes of Health. I had to collect more information on the biochemistry of sickle cell anemia in order to determine a compound that might reverse sickling.

I look back now and wonder if I had been set up all along. The head of the hematology department had another student working in the lab on blood typing; he also did not appear to be a person who did not know what was going on in his lab. Over the next months, I spent hours, Saturdays and Sundays at the Illinois Institute of Technology library. I wrote to the National Institutes of Health and they wrote back to me and sent scientific papers! I struggled through original scientific articles that discussed theories about why cells sickled, why the sickle-cell trait could sometimes be dangerous, and the effects of low concentrations of oxygen and temperatures on hemoglobin S. These were the circumstances under which the red blood cells changed shape. And I learned that Dr. Linus Pauling, called the father of modern day biochemistry, earned the Nobel Prize for his work showing that sickle cell anemia disease was caused by the substitution of a single valine amino acid molecule in the sixth position of the normal hemoglobin amino acid sequence. That single substitution causes all the problems. Through this discovery, Dr. Pauling was able to demonstrate that it is the linear sequence of amino acids that determines the 3-D shape of a protein and its physiologic function. Cool. And I didn't know people actually studied black folks' disease. Here was one study fundamental to understanding modern biochemistry.

Through discussion with the physician, I decided on a compound to test that might inhibit sickling. And we tested it! All of this information I had to find and digest. Many times I had to learn other stuff just to really understand one sentence in a medical journal article. I was jazzed!

Then the head of hematology demanded to see my exhibit for the science fair. He also required me to write and type (no computers or word processors available in those days) a scientific paper. It was most embarrassing when he, a non-native speaker of English, once corrected my spelling—I bet him and lost. I learned about art transfer letters, how to get photographs from microscopes, and statistics. Whew! He was tough and did not accept "pretty" good. He expected excellence. Period. Nothing less. I was surprised that this European doctor showed so much interest in my work, and allowed me to work in his lab. He seemed to really want me to work in his lab. While I was occasionally intimidated by his knowledge and the task, I always spoke up and would try even harder to be prepared the next time. At fourteen and fifteen, I was comfortable being accepted as his colleague.

Perhaps the most lasting impression of this experience is that my taking a chance of being hung up on, refused, and failing put me in touch with people willing to take that same chance on me. Sucking up my feelings of "Wow, can I do this?" and just trying, risking, and being willing to put in the effort to accomplish the task led the way to one of the most positive and enabling experiences in my entire life.

Oh, yeah. I almost forgot about what started all of this. What happened at the science fair? I got an "Excellent" at the City Wide Chicago Public School Science Fair. As a result I was invited to an exhibit at a city wide private school science fair as the public school representative and I won first place.

Introduction to

Ben Carson

I began to ask myself, What is it that I ought to be doing? What am I really good at? I started seriously evaluating my gifts and talents—an important step when choosing a career. I thought, I'm really good at things that require eye-hand coordination. I'm a very careful person. . . . I would make a fabulous brain surgeon.

A brainy idea for sure, but one that would have been called crazy for a destitute, "dumb kid" in Detroit, says Dr. Ben Carson. In his book, *The Big Picture*, this neurosurgeon tells how he changed from that dumb kid with poor expectations to one of the smartest in his school. His mother, who was unable to read, insisted that her sons read two books a week "or else." What was first seen as a punishment was soon transformed to a love of reading for young Ben and a thirst for information.

Carson now spends much of his spare time talking to educators and inner-city kids, telling his own story and encouraging them to raise their expectations. "Work hard" is his message. "Poverty need not be the barrier to a good education and success," he insists.

Carson has received many honorary degrees. One of his outstanding achievements was successfully separating Siamese twin babies attached at the skull.

Carson is currently the director of pediatric neurosurgery at the Johns Hopkins Hospital in Baltimore, Maryland.

Ben Carson
from The Big Picture

Of course, if you had seen me as a youngster and someone had told you that this guy would go on to be a brain surgeon, you might have laughed yourself to death. I was perhaps the worst student you can imagine. In fact, my nickname was *Dummy*.

I remember once having an argument with several of my classmates over who was the dumbest person in the class. It really wasn't much of an argument. Everyone agreed it was me. But when somebody tried to extend that argument to who was the dumbest person in the world, I took exception. We debated vigorously about that.

The teacher gave us a math quiz later that day. As usual I got a zero. And back in those days, you passed your test to the person behind you, and they would correct it as the teacher read out the answers. After you received your graded paper back, you had to report your score, out loud, when the teacher called your name.

Sitting in my seat that day, I stared in despair at the big goose egg at the top of my paper. I began to wonder how in the world I would give the teacher my score without letting all those kids I'd been arguing with know I made a zero.

I began to scheme. I thought, *Maybe if I mumble, she will misinterpret what I say.* So when the teacher called my name, I softly muttered, "Nnnne."

The teacher exclaimed, "Nine! Benjamin, you got nine right? How wonderful! Class, can you see what Benjamin has done? Didn't I tell you if you just applied yourself you could do it? Oh, I am so happy! This is a wonderful day." And she ranted and raved for about five minutes.

The test had thirty questions—but nine right was so much better than my usual grade that the teacher went on and on.

Finally the girl behind me couldn't take it. She stood up and said, "He said, 'None.' " The rest of the kids just roared at that and the teacher was so embarrassed she just sat down. And if I could have disappeared into thin air, never to be heard from again in the history of the world, I would gladly have done so.

But I couldn't. I had to sit there and act like it didn't bother me—even though it did. Not enough to make me study, but it did bother me. Significantly. I remember my midterm report card in that class. I was doing so poorly I failed almost every subject.

My poor mother was mortified. Here she was, with a third-grade education, working two or three jobs at a time as a domestic, cleaning other people's houses, knowing that life didn't hold much for her. And seeing my brother and me going down the same road.

She didn't know what to do. So she prayed and asked God to give her wisdom. What could she do to get her young sons to understand the importance of education so that they could determine their own destinies?

God gave her the wisdom—though my brother and I didn't think it was all that wise. It was to turn off the television. From that point on she would let us watch our choice of only two or three television programs during the week. With all that spare time, we were to read two books a week from the Detroit Public Library and submit to her written book reports. Which she couldn't read. But we didn't know that.

I was extraordinarily unhappy about this new arrangement. All my friends were outside, having a good time. I remember my mother's friends coming to her and saying, "You can't keep boys in the house reading. Boys are supposed to be outside playing and developing their muscles. When they grow up, they'll hate you. They will be sissies. You can't do that!"

Sometimes I would overhear this and I would say, "Listen to them, Mother." But she would never listen. We were going to have to read those books.

Sometimes, when I tell this story, people come up to me afterward and ask, "How was your mother able to get you to read those books? I can't get my kids to read or to ever turn off the television or Nintendo."

I just have to chuckle and say, "Well, back in those days, the parents ran the house. They didn't have to get permission from the kids." That seems to be a novel concept to a lot of people these days.

At any rate, I started reading. And the nice thing was my mother did not dictate what we had to read. I loved animals, so I read every animal book in the Detroit Public Library. And when I finished those, I went on to plants. When I finished those, I went on to rocks because we lived in a dilapidated section of the city near the railroad tracks. And what is there along railroad tracks, but rocks? I would collect little boxes of rocks and take them home and get out my geology book. I would study until I could name virtually every rock, tell how it was formed, and identify where it came from.

Months passed. I was still in fifth grade. Still the dummy in the class. Nobody knew about my reading project.

One day the fifth-grade science teacher walked in and held up a big shiny black rock. He asked, "Can anybody tell me what this is?"

Keep in mind that I never raised my hand. I never answered questions. So I waited for some of the smart kids to raise their hands. None of them did. So I waited for some of the dumb kids to raise their hands. When none of them did, I thought, *This is my big chance.* So I raised my hand . . . and everyone turned around to look. Some of my classmates were poking each other and whispering, "Look, look, Carson's got his hand up. This is gonna be good!"

They couldn't wait to see what was going to happen. And the teacher was shocked. He said, "Benjamin?"

I said, "Mr. Jaeck . . . that's obsidian." And there was silence in the room. Because it sounded good. But no one knew whether it was right or wrong. So the other kids didn't know if they should laugh or be impressed.

Finally the teacher broke the silence and said, "That's right! This is obsidian."

I went on to explain, "Obsidian is formed after a volcanic eruption. Lava flows down and when it hits water there is a super-cooling process. The elements coalesce, air is forced out, the surface glazes over, and . . ."

I suddenly realized everyone was staring at me in amazement. They couldn't believe all this geological information spewing from the mouth of the dummy. But you know, I was perhaps the most amazed person in the room, because it dawned on me in that moment that I was no dummy.

I thought, *Carson, the reason you knew the answer is because you were reading those books. What if you read books about all your subjects—science, math, history, geography, social studies? Couldn't you then know more than all these students who tease you and call you a dummy?* I must admit the idea appealed to me— to the extent that no book was safe from my grasp. I read everything I could get my hands on. If I had five minutes, I had a book. If I was in the bathroom, I was reading a book. If I was waiting for the bus, I was reading a book.

Within a year and a half, I went from the bottom of the class to the top of the class—much to the consternation of all those students who used to tease me and call me Dummy. The same ones would come to me in seventh grade to ask, "Hey, Benny, how do you work this problem?" And I would say, "Sit at my feet, youngster, while I instruct you."

I was perhaps a little bit obnoxious. But after all those years it felt so good to say that to those who had tormented me.

The important point here is that I had the same brain when I was still at the bottom of the class as I had when I reached the top of the class.

The difference was this: in the fifth grade, I thought I was dumb so I acted like I was dumb, and I achieved like a dumb person. As a seventh grader I thought I was smart, so I acted and achieved accordingly. So what does that say about what a person thinks about his own abilities? What does this say about the importance of our self-image? What does it say about the incredible potential of the human brain our Creator has given us?

Think about it. No computer on earth can come close to the capacity of the average human brain. This brain that we all have is a tremendous gift from God—the most complex organ system in the entire universe. Your brain can take in two million bytes of information per second. If this room were completely full and ten times larger than it is, I could bring one of you up here on stage and have you look out at the crowd for one second and lead you away. Fifty years later I could perform an operation, take off the cranial bone, put in some depth electrodes, stimulate the appropriate area, and this person could remember not only where everyone was sitting, but what they were wearing.

That's how amazing and complex the human brain is. It's literally mind-boggling if you study the human brain. Yet we have people walking around talking about what they can't do.

Introduction to

Richard Feynman

I didn't get to do as much as I wanted to, because my mother kept putting me out all the time, to play. But I was often in the house fiddling with my lab.

I bought radios at rummage sales. I didn't have any money, but it wasn't very expensive—they were old, broken radios, and I'd buy them and try to fix them. Usually they were broken in some simpleminded way—some obvious wire was hanging loose, or a coil was broken or partly unwound.

Richard Feynman, who won a Nobel Prize in physics in 1965, grew up in what he liked to call *a small town called Far Rockaway*, actually a part of New York City. In the 1920s, it was a largely Jewish neighborhood of rooming houses and small hotels. His book *Surely You're Joking, Mr. Feynman!* tells of his picaresque, roguish adventures as a boy with an insatiable curiosity. At age eleven Feynman was playing with fuses and coils : . . . and fixing broken radios.

At seventeen Feynman entered the Massachusetts Institute of Technology. Four years later he enrolled in Princeton, where he started work on the Manhattan Project, continuing at Los Alamos to help build the first atomic bomb. After the Second World War, having finished his Ph.D., Feynman taught at Cornell University, and later, as a theoretical physicist, at the California Institute of Technology. Along with his fellow physicist Dr. Murray Gell-Mann, he hypothesized the existence of the quark, and they shared the Nobel Prize for their theory on quantum electrodynamics.

Richard Feynman

from Surely You're Joking,
Mr. Feynman!

One day I was playing with the Ford coil, punching holes in paper with the sparks, and the paper caught on fire. Soon I couldn't hold it any more because it was burning near my fingers, so I dropped it in a metal wastebasket, which had a lot of newspapers in it. Newspapers burn fast, you know, and the flame looked pretty big inside the room. I shut the door so my mother—who was playing bridge with some friends in the living room—wouldn't find out there was a fire in my room, took a magazine that was lying nearby, and put it over the wastebasket to smother the fire.

After the fire was out I took the magazine off, but now the room began to fill up with smoke. The wastebasket was still too hot to handle, so I got a pair of pliers, carried it across the room, and held it out the window for the smoke to blow out.

But because it was breezy outside, the wind lit the fire again, and now the magazine was out of reach. So I pulled the flaming wastebasket back in through the window to get the magazine, and I noticed there were curtains in the window— it was very dangerous!

Well, I got the magazine, put the fire out again, and this time kept the magazine with me while I shook the glowing coals out of the wastepaper basket onto the street, two or three floors below. Then I went out of my room, closed the door behind me, and said to my mother, "I'm going out to play," and the smoke went out slowly through the windows.

I also did some things with electric motors and built an amplifier for a photo cell that I bought that could make a bell ring when I put my hand in front of the cell. I didn't get to do as much as I wanted to, because my mother kept putting me out all the time, to play. But I was often in the house, fiddling with my lab.

I bought radios at rummage sales. I didn't have any money, but it wasn't very expensive—they were old, broken radios, and I'd buy them and try to fix them. Usually they were broken in some simpleminded way—some obvious wire was hanging loose, or a coil was broken or partly unwound—so I could get some of them going. On one of these radios one night I got WACO in Waco, Texas—it was tremendously exciting!

On this same tube radio up in my lab I was able to hear a station up in Schenectady called WGN. Now, all of us kids— my two cousins, my sister, and the neighborhood kids— listened on the radio downstairs to a program called the "Eno Crime Club"—Eno effervescent salts—it was *the* thing! Well, I

126

discovered that I could hear this program up in my lab on WGN one hour before it was broadcast in New York! So I'd discover what was going to happen, and then, when we were all sitting around the radio downstairs listening to the "Eno Crime Club," I'd say, "You know, we haven't heard from so-and-so in a long time. I betcha he comes and saves the situation."

Two seconds later, *bup-bup*, he comes! So they all got excited about this, and I predicted a couple of other things. Then they realized that there must be some trick to it—that I must know, somehow. So I owned up to what it was, that I could hear it upstairs the hour before.

You know what the result was, naturally. Now they couldn't wait for the regular hour. They all had to sit upstairs in my lab with this little creaky radio for half an hour, listening to the "Eno Crime Club" from Schenectady.

We lived at that time in a big house; it was left by my grandfather to his children, and they didn't have much money aside from the house. It was a very large, wooden house, and I would run wires all around the outside, and had plugs in all the rooms, so I could always listen to my radios, which were upstairs in my lab. I also had a loudspeaker—not the whole speaker, but the part without the big horn on it.

One day, when I had my earphones on, I connected them to the loudspeaker, and I discovered something: I put my finger in the speaker and I could hear it in the earphones; I scratched the speaker and I'd hear it in the earphones. So I discovered that the speaker could act like a microphone, and you didn't even need any batteries. At school we were talking about Alexander Graham Bell, so I gave a demonstration of the speaker and the earphones. I didn't know it at the time but I think it was the type of telephone he originally used.

So now I had a microphone, and I could broadcast from upstairs to downstairs, and from downstairs to upstairs, using the amplifiers of my rummage-sale radios. At that time my sister Joan, who was nine years younger than I was, must have been about two or three, and there was a guy on the radio called Uncle Don that she liked to listen to. He'd sing little songs about "good children," and so on, and he'd read cards sent in by parents telling that "Mary So-and-so is having a birthday this Saturday at 25 Flatbush Avenue."

One day my cousin Francis and I sat Joan down and said that there was a special program she should listen to. Then we ran upstairs and we started to broadcast: "This is Uncle Don. We know a very nice little girl named Joan who lives on New Broadway; she's got a birthday coming—not today, but such-and-such. She's a cute girl." We sang a little song, and then we made music: "*Deedle leet deet, doodle doodle loot doot; deedle deedle leet, doodle loot doot doo . . .*" We went through the whole deal, and then we came downstairs: "How was it? Did you like the program?"

"It was good," she said, "but why did you make the music with your mouth?"

One day I got a telephone call: "Mister, are you Richard Feynman?"

"Yes."

"This is a hotel. We have a radio that doesn't work, and would like it repaired. We understand you might be able to do something about it."

"But I'm only a little boy," I said. "I don't know how—"

"Yes, we know that, but we'd like you to come over anyway."

It was a hotel that my aunt was running, but I didn't know that. I went over there with—they still tell the story—a big screwdriver in my back pocket. Well, I was small, so *any* screwdriver looked big in my back pocket.

I went up to the radio and tried to fix it. I didn't know anything about it, but there was also a handyman at the hotel, and either he noticed, or I noticed, a loose knob on the rheostat—to turn up the volume—so that it wasn't turning the shaft. He went off and filed something, and fixed it up so it worked.

The next radio I tried to fix didn't work at all. That was easy: it wasn't plugged in right. As the repair jobs got more and more complicated, I got better and better, and more elaborate. I bought myself a milliammeter in New York and converted it into a voltmeter that had different scales on it by using the right lengths (which I calculated) of very fine copper wire. It wasn't very accurate, but it was good enough to tell whether things were in the right ballpark at different connections in those radio sets.

The main reason people hired me was the Depression. They didn't have any money to fix their radios, and they'd hear about this kid who would do it for less. So I'd climb on roofs to fix antennas, and all kinds of stuff. I got a series of lessons of ever-increasing difficulty. Ultimately I got some job like converting a DC set into an AC set, and it was very hard to keep the hum from going through the system, and I didn't build it quite right. I shouldn't have bitten that one off, but I didn't know.

One job was really sensational. I was working at the time for a printer, and a man who knew that printer knew I was trying to get jobs fixing radios, so he sent a fellow around to the print shop to pick me up. The guy is obviously poor—his car is a complete wreck—and we go to his house, which is in a cheap part of town. On the way, I say, "What's the trouble with the radio?"

He says, "When I turn it on it makes a noise, and after a while the noise stops and everything's all right, but I don't like the noise at the beginning."

I think to myself: "What the hell! If he hasn't got any money, you'd think he could stand a little noise for a while."

And all the time, on the way to his house, he's saying things like, "Do you know anything about radios? How do you know about radios—you're just a little boy!"

He's putting me down the whole way, and I'm thinking, "So what's the matter with him? So it makes a little noise."

But when we got there I went over to the radio and turned it on. Little noise? *My God!* No wonder the poor guy couldn't stand it. The thing began to roar and wobble—WUH BUH BUH BUH BUH—A *tremendous* amount of noise. Then it quieted down and played correctly. So I started to think: "How can that happen?"

I start walking back and forth, thinking, and I realize that one way it can happen is that the tubes are heating up in the wrong order—that is, the amplifier's all hot, the tubes are ready to go, and there's nothing feeding in, or there's some back circuit feeding in, or something wrong in the beginning part—the RF part—and therefore it's making a lot of noise, picking up something. And when the RF circuit's finally going, and the grid voltages are adjusted, everything's all right.

So the guy says, "What are you doing? You come to fix the radio, but you're only walking back and forth!"

I say, "I'm thinking!" Then I said to myself, "All right, take the tubes out, and reverse the order completely in the set." (Many radio sets in those days used the same tubes in different places—212's, I think they were, or 212-A's.) So I changed the tubes around, stepped to the front of the radio, turned the thing on, and it's as quiet as a lamb: it waits until it heats up, and then plays perfectly—no noise.

When a person has been negative to you, and then you do something like that, they're usually a hundred percent the other way, kind of to compensate. He got me other jobs, and kept telling everybody what a tremendous genius I was, saying, "He fixes radios by *thinking*!" The whole idea of thinking, to fix a radio—a little boy stops and thinks, and figures out how to do it—he never thought that was possible.

Introduction to

Edward O. Wilson

Edward Wilson's interest in the abundance of life outdoors, from the tiniest insects to monster whales, began as a boy. His nomadic life made nature his companion, because, he said, it was one part of his world that would always be there, a part of life he believed was rock steady.

When his parents separated, he moved from Florida to Alabama to Virginia to Maryland, attending fourteen different schools. He never stayed long enough to belong anywhere. Most of his free time was spent alone observing and exploring the marvels of wildlife. By the time he completed high school, Wilson had developed a passion for studying biologic diversity that lasted a lifetime.

From his description of himself as a boy on Paradise Beach in Florida, we feel the sense of wonder he first experienced . . . and never lost.

It was on the same Paradise Beach that he lost the vision in one eye in a freakish fishing accident, which made him change from studying general ecology to entymology. Minute crawling and flying insects could be easily observed with his good eye.

After receiving his Ph.D. at Harvard, Wilson devoted his time to teaching, research, and writing, and he is now noted for his uncanny ability to clarify the principles of evolutionary biology for the ordinary reader.

Edward O. Wilson
from Paradise Beach

What happened, what we *think* happened in distant memory, is built around a small collection of dominating images. In one of my own from the age of seven, I stand in the shallows off Paradise Beach, staring down at a huge jellyfish in water so still and clear that its every detail is revealed as though it were trapped in glass. The creature is astonishing. It existed outside my previous imagination. I study it from every angle I can manage from above the water's surface. Its opalescent pink bell is divided by thin red lines that radiate from center to circular edge. A wall of tentacles falls from the rim to surround and partially veil a feeding tube and other organs, which fold in and out like the fabric of a drawn curtain. I can see only a little way into this lower tissue mass. I want to know more but am afraid to wade in deeper and look more closely into the heart of the creature.

The jellyfish, I know now, was a sea nettle, *Chrysoora*, a

scyphozoan, a medusa, a member of the pelagic fauna that drifted in from the Gulf of Mexico and paused in the place I found it. I had no idea then of these names from the lexicon of zoology. The only word I had heard was *jellyfish*. But what a spectacle my animal was, and how inadequate, how demeaning, the bastard word used to label it. I should have been able to whisper its true name: *scyph-o-zo-an!* Think of it! I have found a scyphozoan. The name would have been a more fitting monument to this discovery.

The creature hung there motionless for hours. As evening approached and the time came for me to leave, its tangled undermass appeared to stretch deeper into the darkening water. Was this, I wondered, an animal or a collection of animals? Today I can say that it was a single animal. And that another outwardly similar animal found in the same waters, the Portuguese man-of-war, is a colony of animals so tightly joined as to form one smoothly functioning superorganism. Such are the general facts I recite easily now, but this sea nettle was special. It came into my world abruptly, from I knew not where, radiating what I cannot put into words except—*alien purpose and dark happenings in the kingdom of deep water*. The scyphozoan still embodies, when I summon its image, all the mystery and tensed malignity of the sea.

The next morning the sea nettle was gone. I never saw another during that summer of 1936. The place, Paradise Beach, which I have revisited in recent years, is a small settlement on the east shore of Florida's Perdido Bay, not far from Pensacola and in sight of Alabama across the water.

There was trouble at home in this season of fantasy. My parents were ending their marriage that year. Existence was difficult for them, but not for me, their only child, at least not yet. I had been placed in the care of a family that boarded one or two boys during the months the summer vacation. Paradise Beach was paradise truly named for a little boy. Each morning after breakfast I left the small shorefront house to wander alone in search of treasures along the strand. I waded in and out of the dependably warm surf and scrounged for anything I could find in the drift. Sometimes I just sat on a rise to scan the open water. Back in time for lunch, out again, back for dinner, out once again, and, finally, off to bed to relive my continuing adventure briefly before falling asleep.

I have no remembrance of the names of the family I stayed with, what they looked like, their ages, or even how many there were. Most likely they were a married couple and, I am willing to suppose, caring and warmhearted people. They have passed out of my memory, and I have no need to learn their identity. It was the animals of that place that cast a lasting spell. I was seven years old, and every species, large and small, was a wonder to be examined, thought about, and, if possible, captured and examined again.

There were needlefish, foot-long green torpedoes with slender beaks, cruising the water just beneath the surface. Nervous in temperament, they kept you in sight and never let you come close enough to reach out a hand and catch them. I

136

wondered where they went at night, but never found out. Blue crabs with skin-piercing claws scuttled close to shore at dusk. Easily caught in long-handled nets, they were boiled and cracked open and eaten straight or added to gumbo, the spicy seafood stew of the Gulf coast.

How I longed to discover animals each larger than the last, until finally I caught a glimpse of some true giant! I knew there were large animals out there in deep water. Occasionally a school of bottlenose porpoises passed offshore less than a stone's throw from where I stood. In pairs, trios, and quartets they cut the surface with their backs and dorsal fins, arced down and out of sight, and broke the water again ten or twenty yards farther on. Their repetitions were so rhythmic that I could pick the spot where they would appear next. On calm days I sometimes scanned the glassy surface of Perdido Bay for hours at a time in the hope of spotting something huge and monstrous as it rose to the surface. I wanted at least to see a shark, to watch the fabled dorsal fin thrust proud out of the water, knowing it would look a lot like a porpoise at a distance but would surface and sound at irregular intervals. I also hoped for more than sharks, what exactly I could not say: something to enchant the rest of my life.

Almost all that came in sight were clearly porpoises, but I was not completely disappointed. Before I tell you about the one exception, let me say something about the psychology of monster hunting. Giants exist as a state of the mind. They are defined not as an absolute measurement but as a proportionality. I estimate that when I was seven years old I saw animals at about twice the size I see them now. The bell of a sea nettle averages ten inches across, I know that now; but the one I found seemed two feet across—a grown man's two feet. So giants can be real, even if adults don't choose to classify them as such. I was destined to meet such a creature at last. But it would not appear as a swirl on the surface of the open water.

It came close in at dusk, suddenly, as I sat on the dock leading away from shore to the family boathouse raised on pilings in shallow water. In the failing light I could barely see to the bottom, but I stayed perched on the dock anyway, looking for any creature large or small that might be moving. Without warning a gigantic ray, many times larger than the stingrays of common experience, glided silently out of the darkness, beneath my dangling feet, and away into the depths on the other side. It was gone in seconds, a circular shadow, seeming to blanket the whole bottom. I was thunderstruck.

Why do I tell you this little boy's story of medusas, rays, and sea monsters, nearly sixty years after the fact? Because it illustrates, I think, how a naturalist is created. A child comes to the edge of deep water with a mind prepared for wonder. He is like a primitive adult of long ago, an acquisitive early *Homo* arriving at the shore of Lake Malawi, say, or the Mozambique Channel. The experience must have been repeated countless times over thousands of generations, and it was richly rewarded.

Introduction to

Dean Kamen

Invention is predominantly individualistic. Everything . . . comes from the lone worker who follows the fleeting inspiration of a moment and finally does something that has not been done before.

This quote is from the inventor of a three-phase motor, Nikola Tesla. It fits the description in every respect of Dean Kamen, the owner of more than one hundred patents.

As a young teenager in Rockville Center, New York, one of four children, whose father was a comic book artist and his mother a schoolteacher, Dean started tinkering with sound and light boxes in his bedroom, "which caused lights to go off and on, and deafening sound to come from his radio," said his mother.

Their indulgent parents allowed Dean and his older brother Barton to experiment, raising as many as one hundred live rats and to set up a workshop in their basement on Long Island.

Dean stocked the basement laboratory with machinery to help create new audio/visual equipment. This led to his first patent and a sizable financial reward while still in high school. Later, after leaving Worcester Polytechnic Institute (where he didn't bother to finish his degree), Dean started his own company in an old factory in Farmingdale, New York. One invention followed another, all of them huge successes that were sold throughout the world. Two of Kamen's more recent inventions are the Ibot, a wheelchair that can safely climb stairs, and a self-balancing scooter, called the Segway. The Segway is battery powered and contains five gyroscopes that keep it balanced under almost any circumstance. Kamen believes it may change the way people move around in crowded cities, reducing the amount of car traffic and auto emissions in many parts of the world.

Dean Kamen
On Becoming an Inventor

When I was twelve years old and Barton, my older brother, was around fifteen, we took over the family basement. At first, I made a darkroom for developing pictures, and Bart was using it as his lab where he was raising about one hundred white rats, removing their thymus glands, and trying to figure out the glands' dysfunction. He wanted pictures taken of his experiment, doing the surgery on rats, and since I already had a darkroom, I took the pictures, though somewhat reluctantly. I didn't like the blood.

Then Bart went off to college and I had use of the rest of the basement. I stopped doing photography and became interested in electronics. It was the early days of disco, when making music and light shows was the rage. Everyone wanted to buy a box that could connect to their stereo to create new light and sound effects. I started building boxes after school, buying components from a nearby Radio Shack, and reading up on electronic recipes for building loaders in the basement workshop. I began buying voltmeters, soldering irons, and other tools for making light organs to sell at school and in my neighborhood. I made enough money to stock more and more equipment in the family basement.

Then I heard about a summer job through my uncle who was a dentist. He introduced me to one of his patients who had a business selling audio-visual equipment for big light and music shows. He was looking for some new, better equipment. I spent all summer when I was sixteen building high-powered light-controlled systems that synchronized many Kodak projectors at once, as many as sixty-four to 120 of them, and reduced the cumbersome machines from the size of a refrigerator to the size of a toaster. Not only was this invention used in theaters, but it was sold to the Museum of Natural History and the New York Planetarium to project views of the heavens on the ceiling. To make this new device I had bought every kind of electrical equipment I could find, and still had money left over.

My next challenge was that I wanted to make things out of metal, so I became interested in how to use a lathe, a milling machine, and so on. I went to buy this new equipment I thought I'd need and met a man who had a machine shop of his own who was about to retire and move to Florida. He allowed me to visit him after school and on weekends to observe how he used all his tools. I was hooked. When he retired I bought not only all his big equipment but all his little toolboxes as well—they were treasures!

I decided to put his entire machine shop in our basement, but there were two problems. . . . One, his shop wouldn't fit in our basement, and two, there was no way the lathe, weighing fifteen hundred pounds, and the milling machine, weighing two thousand pounds, could be carried into the basement. I solved this problem by hiring a contractor to dig a large hole, break open a wall of the basement, enclose the addition with concrete, and add a roof that could be used for building an outside deck to the house. I also enlarged my mother's kitchen and pantry. I now had the entire machine shop in our basement. At the time I was making enough money from my electronic devices to pay for all of this.

From this well-stocked basement came a whole new set of really neat projects. My younger brother, Mitch, and his friends, as well as some of my own friends, would come after school to help. At sixteen I was now a young entrepreneur, paying them for their help. I was surprised by the number of orders I was getting for more and more equipment. Soon I didn't have time to build and design new things. Giving over this work to other kids gave me more time to do what I *wanted* to do. This went on after school and all summer long.

I had just finished making a complicated piece of equipment that was to be used for a show opening in Philadelphia called "Fiorello." When the machine arrived they had trouble wiring it, so instead of going off to college that morning for an orientation, I spent several days at the theater fixing my light/sound equipment. The show received poor reviews, except for the mention by one reviewer of the "special effects," which, he wrote, were "outstanding."

I then registered at Worcester Polytechnic Institute. It was 1969. I spent every weekend at home to keep my successful business going. At college I was struck by how smart the teachers were—in electronics, in physics, and in mathematics. I was intimidated by the huge buildings devoted to these studies, the knowledge I needed and wanted to gain. I found that at college I could get help from my teachers with solving business problems and in learning new techniques for designing new things. I enjoyed talking to my professors and learning physics and other complex subjects—*but I* never *had time to go to class.* I literally never went to class. My professors were mentors and private tutors. The professors gave me as much time as they reasonably could. Every once in a while one would say, "Sorry, I've got to go teach a class"—and leave.

I didn't officially *graduate* from Worcester Polytechnic Institute until years later when I was awarded their honorary Ph.D. By then I'd created and patented many successful inventions.

Maybe it was my brother Bart's interest in medical problems that propelled me into a whole new direction—not projectors or sound equipment, but the enhancement of medical devices used around the world to help those with serious and chronic illnesses such as diabetes, thalassemia, and more. For some patients, having such an illness meant spending days in a hospital being hooked up to elaborate equipment that pumped medication into their bloodstreams. While still in college and working in my basement lab every weekend for many hours, I invented my first medical device to keep blocked heart arteries open with a tiny stent, which eliminated the need for angioplasty in many patients.

I can't say how inventions happen. Sometimes you look at the same thing everyone looks at—and then end up seeing something different.

BUSINESS AND POLITICS

Politics is called a game—but a serious one.
Business is another kind of challenge requiring
courage, skill, and intelligence. The stories of
successful businessmen and politicians are often
remarkable and inspiring. Read on.

Introduction to

Nelson Mandela

In 1964 everyone thought that political activist Nelson Mandela would remain in jail for the rest of his life. His fight against apartheid in South Africa, the forced separation of blacks and "colored" into designated areas, had started soon after he finished law school. It continued despite harassment and numerous arrests. He was sentenced to life in prison for heading the outlawed African National Congress. Little did his accusers know or expect that one day Mandela would become the president of their country.

Nelson (Rolihlahla) Mandela was born in 1918 in Umtata, on the eastern cape of South Africa. He was the son of a counselor to the king of the Thembu tribe. The death of his father when Nelson was nine profoundly changed his way of life and how he perceived himself and his future.

Mandela attended the Methodist Mission Center school, in Healdtown, then enrolled in University College at Fort Hare.

He was expelled two years later for his role in a student strike.

Mandela came to believe that the best way to combat the restrictive laws against black Africans was through public protest. After receiving a law degree from the University of South Africa he used his knowledge of law to change the status quo in a country where law was used as a weapon of oppression. But years of nonviolent protest proved to have little or no effect. After the massacre in Sharpeville in which sixty-nine demonstrators were killed and hundreds more injured, Mandela abandoned legal means. He formed an organization that carried out acts of sabotage to undermine the entrenched system.

For twenty-seven years Mandela was held prisoner, though supporters from all over the world demanded his release. In 1990, succumbing to international pressure, South Africa's President F. W. De Klerk became convinced of Mandela's integrity and desire to maintain democracy in South Africa. He ordered that Mandela be pardoned and freed from prison.

Shortly thereafter, one of the most momentous elections in all of Africa took place. A new constitution was adopted for South Africa ordering the end of apartheid, and Nelson Mandela was overwhelmingly elected president of his country.

Nelson Mandela

from Long Walk to Freedom

One night, when I was nine years old, I was aware of a commotion in the household. My father, who took turns visiting his wives and usually came to us for perhaps one week a month, had arrived. But it was not at his accustomed time, for he was not scheduled to be with us for another few days. I found him in my mother's hut, lying on his back on the floor, in the midst of what seemed like an endless fit of coughing. Even to my young eyes, it was clear that my father was not long for this world. He was ill with some type of lung disease, but it was not diagnosed, as my father had never visited a doctor. He remained in the hut for several days without moving or speaking, and then one night he took a turn for the worse. My mother and my father's youngest wife, Nodayimani, who had come to stay with us, were looking after him, and late that night he called for Nodayimani. "Bring me my tobacco," he told her. My mother and Nodayimani conferred, and decided that it was unwise that he have tobacco in his current state. But he persisted in calling for it, and eventually Nodayimani filled his pipe, lit it, and then handed it to him. My father smoked and became calm. He continued smoking for perhaps an hour, and then, his pipe still lit, he died.

I do not remember experiencing great grief so much as feeling cut adrift. Although my mother was the center of my existence, I defined myself through my father. My father's passing changed my whole life in a way that I did not suspect at the time. After a brief period of mourning, my mother informed me that I would be leaving Qunu. I did not ask her why, or where I was going.

I packed the few things that I possessed, and early one morning we set out on a journey westward to my new residence. I mourned less for my father than for the world I was leaving behind. Qunu was all that I knew, and I loved it in the unconditional way that a child loves his first home. Before we disappeared behind the hills, I turned and looked for what I imagined was the last time at my village.

We traveled by foot and in silence until the sun was sinking slowly toward the horizon. But the silence of the heart between mother and child is not a lonely one. My mother and I never talked very much, but we did not need to. I never doubted her love or questioned her support. It was an exhausting journey, along rocky dirt roads, up and down hills, past numerous villages, but we did not pause. Late in the afternoon, at the bottom of a shallow valley surrounded by trees, we came upon a village at the center of which was a large and gracious home that so far exceeded anything that I had ever seen that all I could do was marvel at it. The buildings consisted of two *iingxande* (rectangular houses) and seven stately *rondavels* (superior huts), all washed in white lime, dazzling even in the light of the setting sun. There was a large front garden and a maize field bordered by rounded peach trees. An even more spacious garden spread out in back, which boasted apple trees, a vegetable garden, a strip of flowers, and a patch of wattles. Nearby was a white stucco church.

In the shade of two gum trees that graced the doorway of the front of the main house sat a group of about twenty tribal elders. Encircling the property, contentedly grazing on the rich land, was a herd of at least fifty cattle and perhaps five hundred sheep. Everything was beautifully tended, and it was a vision of wealth and order beyond my imagination. This was the Great Place, Mqhekezweni, the provisional capital of Thembuland, the royal residence of Chief Jongintaba Dalindyebo, acting regent of the Thembu people.

As I contemplated all this grandeur, an enormous motorcar rumbled through the western gate and the men sitting in the shade immediately arose. They doffed their hats and then jumped to their feet shouting. *"Boyese a-a-a, Jongintaba!"* (Hail, Jongintaba!), the traditional salute of the Xhosas for their chief. Out of the motorcar (I learned later that this majestic vehicle was a Ford V8) stepped a short, thickset man wearing a smart suit. I could see that he had the confidence and bearing of a man who was used to the exercise of authority. His name suited him, for Jongintaba literally means "One who looks at the mountain," and he was a man with a sturdy presence toward whom all eyes gazed. He had a dark complexion and an intelligent face, and he casually shook hands with each of the men beneath the tree, men who, as I later discovered, comprised the highest Thembu court of justice. This was the regent who was to become my guardian and benefactor for the next decade.

In that moment of beholding Jongintaba and his court I felt like a sapling pulled root and branch from the earth and flung into the center of a stream whose strong current I could not resist. I felt a sense of awe mixed with bewilderment. Until then I had had no thoughts of anything but my own pleasures, no higher ambition than to eat well and become a champion stick-fighter. I had no thought of money, or class, or fame, or power. Suddenly a new world opened before me. Children from poor homes often find themselves beguiled by a host of new temptations when suddenly confronted by great wealth. I was no exception. I felt many of my established beliefs and loyalties begin to ebb away. The slender foundation built by my parents began to shake. In that instant, I saw that life might hold more for me than being a champion stick-fighter.

I learned later that, in the wake of my father's death, Jongintaba had offered to become my guardian. He would treat me as he treated his other children, and I would have the same advantages as they. My mother had no choice; one did not turn down such an overture from the regent. She was satisfied that although she would miss me, I would have a more advantageous upbringing in the regent's care than in her own. The regent had not forgotten that it was due to my father's intervention that he had become acting paramount chief.

My mother remained in Mqhekezweni for a day or two before returning to Qunu. Our parting was without fuss. She offered no sermons, no words of wisdom, no kisses. I suspect she did not want me to feel bereft at her departure and so was matter-of-fact. I knew that my father had wanted me to be educated and prepared for a wide world, and I could not do that in Qunu. Her tender look was all the affection and support I needed, and as she departed she turned to me and said, "*Uqinisufokotho, Kwedini!*" (Brace yourself, my boy!) Children are often the least sentimental of creatures, especially if they are absorbed in some new pleasure. Even as my dear mother and first friend was leaving, my head was swimming with the delights of my new home. How could I not be braced up? I was already wearing the handsome new outfit purchased for me by my guardian.

I cannot pinpoint a moment when I became politicized, when I knew that I would spend my life in the liberation struggle. To be an African in South Africa means that one is politicized from the moment of one's birth, whether one acknowledges it or not. An African child is born in an Africans Only hospital, taken home in an Africans Only bus, lives in an Africans Only area, and attends Africans Only schools, if he attends school at all.

When he grows up, he can hold Africans Only jobs, rent a house in Africans Only townships, ride Africans Only trains, and be stopped at any time of the day or night and be ordered to produce a pass, failing which he will be arrested and thrown in jail. His life is circumscribed by racist laws and regulations that cripple his growth, dim his potential, and stunt his life. This was the reality, and one could deal with it in a myriad of ways.

I had no epiphany, no singular revelation, no moment of truth, but a steady accumulation of a thousand slights, a thousand indignities, a thousand unremembered moments, produced in me an anger, a rebelliousness, a desire to fight the system that imprisoned my people. There was no particular day on which I said: From henceforth I will devote myself to the liberation of my people; instead, I simply found myself doing so, and could not do otherwise.

Introduction to

Vernon E. Jordan, Jr.

*Looking back on my teenage self, I can see that I was beginning
to come into some sense of who I was going to be. I'd always felt
that I wanted to be a leader—my mother had encouraged this
from the time I was a little boy. Now I was having experiences and
successes that made it clear that I could, in fact, become a leader
in some capacity. The more positive attention I received the more
convinced I became. The only question was, leader of what?*

Vernon E. Jordan, Jr. became a civil rights leader in the
sixties and seventies after receiving a law degree from Howard
University in Washington, D.C.

As a child he experienced all the prejudices of Southern
segregationists, their treatment of "colored folk" as inferior to
white folk. Jordan took up this challenge by applying to a
predominantly white college after completing high school in a
school for "colored" students in Atlanta, Georgia. He was
accepted at DePauw University in Greencastle, Indiana, where

he discovered that *some* whites accepted him as their equal (his two roommates, for example). While studying at DePauw, Jordan earned money during the summer months as a chauffeur for a wealthy old businessman named Robert Maddox, back in Atlanta. It was an all-day job with many hours between lunch and dinner when he was not needed.

Maddox had a wonderful library that soon became a place of refuge for me during the dead hours of the afternoon. Shakespeare, Thoreau, Emerson—it had everything.

When his boss walked into the library one afternoon, he was astounded to find his chauffeur reading. Eighty-year-old Maddox then began to announce to his friends that "Vernon can read," as though it were a bizarre, unlikely thing for a "colored man" to do. It was the memory of just such occasions that prompted Jordan to become actively involved in the civil rights movement.

In 1961 Jordan was a member of the legal team that desegregated the University of Georgia. He also was actively involved with the NAACP (National Association for the Advancement of Colored People) along with Medgar Evers, and later became the executive director of the United Negro College Fund and advisor to President Clinton.

Vernon E. Jordan, Jr.

from Vernon Can Read!

It was through my mother's business that I had my first serious exposure to lawyers. From 1948 until about 1960, my mother catered the monthly dinners of the very exclusive Lawyers Club. The club's elite membership was drawn from the most accomplished (or at least the most socially connected) attorneys in Atlanta.

The atmosphere at the meetings was just about what one would expect: all white, all male, cigar smoke, plenty of good-natured banter, and whiskey, along with my mother's filet mignon wrapped in bacon. I moved among the guests as a servant, quiet and unobtrusive, for the most part ignored. This was not a two-way street. I was a teenager who happened to be intensely interested in the men of that club—how they made their living and how they dealt with one another outside of the public view. Of all the places we worked, weddings, bar mitzvahs, dinners, cocktail parties—you name it, we did it—I think I liked the Lawyers Club the most of all.

In the world as it existed at the time, the thought that I could one day be among those men was beyond far-fetched. And yet I was instantly drawn to the world in which they lived. These were the movers and shakers of their community, for the most part secure in their power and positions. This confidence allowed them to treat one another with an easy camaraderie that was admirable, and which was very instructive for what was to come later in my life. I wanted to be a part of something like that. Not necessarily with those individuals, but with a group of people who were doing similarly important things and who could meet to enjoy one another's company.

I was so interested in their operations that I sometimes neglected my duties. The club always had an after-dinner speaker. Instead of staying in the kitchen, helping to clean up, and getting packed to go home, I would go back near the dining area, stand at a discreet distance, and listen to the speeches. What they were saying did not always interest me, but I was interested in the way each speaker presented himself. It was during that time that I firmly decided that I was going to be a lawyer.

I felt it so deeply, even as I knew that the men whom I served could never in their wildest dreams imagine that I could share a profession with them. But being a waiter was simply a temporary phase for me. I knew what was to come, and what I would one day look like when the change came.

In the meantime, there was my mother's catering business to

work in and other jobs that came my way. As a teenager, I was a camp counselor for part of the summer at the Butler Street YMCA. There is nothing like trying to handle twenty-five eight-year-old boys when it is too rainy to go outside and some way has to be found to harness what amounts to unbridled energy. My hat is off to all the elementary school teachers of the world. I sang so many camp songs, broke up so many fights, cleaned up after so many spills. Then again, I also heard many unintentionally funny comments, saw kids who didn't think they could do things (like learning to swim) become accomplished under the direction of the Y's staff.

For a time, I had a dishwashing job at Emory University, where I worked part-time during the school year and in the summers when I'd finished a session as counselor at the YMCA. I got the job when I was fifteen and kept it for most of my years in high school. This job gave me my first experience in managing people. I was the youngest person on the dishwashing crew, which consisted of older men. I think I may have been the only one there who could really read. In the land of the blind, the one-eyed man is king. So I was made the head of the dishwashing crew because I could read well, and my employer was impressed.

Naturally this caused some resentment. I was young, and they were older. One saving grace was my height. I had a tough time telling them what to do or, at least, having them actually do what I told them to do. The work would pile up, and they'd be downstairs playing cards. Our supervisor, a white woman named Mrs. Haney, was very, very mean. Everyone was afraid of her. When the crew disappeared on me, I'd have to go back and invoke the name of Mrs. Haney to get them back in line. "I don't care whether this gets done," I'd say. "I do know that Mrs. Haney sure does." As a management tool, this was a pretty blunt instrument. But it usually did the trick.

The jobs I held as a teenager reinforced my certainty that I was going to do something different in the world. My co-workers, in all likelihood, were doing some version of what would be their life's work. I was very much aware of the differences in our circumstances, of the fact that I was being prepared (and was preparing myself) to move to the next level. Most of the people who worked with me had little or no education and, therefore, almost no hope of moving anywhere beyond the next job that would be just like the one before.

Following my senior year in high school, I worked as a waiter at the Capital City Country Club in De Kalb County. The captain was a man who was always very busy—nice, but a no-nonsense type of fellow. After working there a while, I noticed the captain followed a curious ritual. As he performed some task, the cashier would read the day's menu to him three times before he began the day's service.

I never thought a thing about this until we went to the filling station one day and there was a contest going on. If you filled the car up, you'd get a prize. The captain had gotten a full tank of gas, so he was eligible to win. When the attendant handed him the form to fill out, he said, a bit too gruffly, "I don't have time for that—give it to my assistant," gesturing in my direction.

Then it hit me: He could not read. That was the point of having the cashier read the daily menu to him. He always claimed it was just a matter of efficiency, that he could keep doing little chores while others read to him. This was just a cover for what must have been a deep embarrassment.

I was embarrassed for him. And I was so sorry at the same time. What a strain it must have been, to go through life memorizing things so you could get through your job, having to hide the fact that you couldn't read to avoid ridicule. It was ingenious, but it was also sad. He was such a proud man. There was no way I could let on I'd learned his secret. So I took the form, filled it out, and we never said another word about it.

My experiences with work during these years not only provided an outlet for my youthful energy—they gave me a sense of power and control over my life. By working and saving my money, I could have a few of the things I wanted. From my view, there was every reason to want to continue in this vein. My mother's sense of the importance of work, entrepreneurship, and frugality colored my whole way of thinking about this, both then and now. Her early experiences in life—the racism, the economic deprivation—evidently caused her to believe that it was important to have a plan in life or others would control your destiny. When we started working, she took my brother Windsor and me to the bank to open our own savings accounts. We had our passbooks, and when we'd get our statements, Mama would note how the interest compounded on our principal. In her view, this was one of the most important lessons in life for us to learn.

I sometimes think it's hard for people who have grown up with the teachings of the church, as most blacks have, to feel entirely comfortable with what might be seen just as the pursuit of money. "It's easier for a camel to fit through the eye of a needle than it is for a rich man to get into the kingdom of heaven," we have been taught, along with "Money is the root of all evil." Even "Blessed are the poor" suggests that a person who wants to make money (beyond what it takes to buy food, clothes, and shelter) is somehow morally suspect.

Of course, there's another reason that some in the black community may feel ambivalent about pursuing money with a lot of energy. It was the naked pursuit of money that brought our ancestors to these shores, chained in the hulls of ships. People used money to buy us. They made money by selling us. Fortunes were built on this activity with no serious thought about the morality of it all. Even if the religious counsel against worshipping Mammon didn't cause a yellow light to flash among our people, history alone would provide a reason for caution.

Although this is understandable, it is ultimately shortsighted. No group in this country can hope to make strides for itself without economic advancement—on an individual level and on a group level. Ruby Hurley, who was my boss when I was Georgia field director for the National Association for the Advancement of Colored People (NAACP), said there were two things that white people understood: the dollar and the ballot. Those interested in maintaining white supremacy worked hard to keep blacks away from both. She was right. Both things have to be attended to if blacks are to make real progress in America and in the world. I have never had any doubt about this at all.

I didn't spend all of my childhood and youth working for pay. My primary occupation was student. I did well in my studies from the very beginning, and I got a reputation in school and in my neighborhood for being smart. This was both good and bad for me.

On the good side, I got to enjoy the positive reinforcement it brought from my teachers, my mother, and other adults. This kind of thing builds on itself. If people tell you that you are smart, you have the confidence and incentive to work to keep that image.

The downside was that there was something of a stigma attached to being too intelligent. Although the stigma affected both girls and boys, it was much worse for boys. I will never forget it. One day when I was in the eighth grade, a girl in our class was writing on the board. She had drawn two columns, with the headings "Girls in our class" and "Boys in our class." She listed everyone's name. At the end of the "Girls" column, she wrote "Vernon."

What was that about? Because I was the best student in the class—I answered the questions, did my homework, tried to please my teachers, spoke correctly—I was a "girl." That kind of thing was meant to hurt, and it did. Not that I thought there was anything wrong with girls. I liked girls very much. I just wasn't one of them. What had I done wrong besides trying to do well in school?

Even my father had a little bit of this in him. I do believe there were times that it bothered him that I was one of the smartest kids in my school. It wasn't that he didn't want me to do well in my studies. He was just suspicious of the enthusiasm I had for it. In his mind, that meant that I was going to grow up to be what he would have called a "sissy."

At the base of all this was fear. If you think of where my father came from and the set of values he brought with him— a real man didn't sit around reading books—this was a foreign thing, having a son who seemed intent on outfitting himself for a world beyond what he knew. I remember once when I was in junior high school, our principal, Mr. Charles Gideons, came to our house for dinner. I heard my father muttering that he was worried about me. Mr. Gideons, who must have been a pretty good student himself to have grown up to be principal of a school, didn't seem concerned at all.

It took a while, but it dawned on my father that being smart and interested in school didn't mean that I was so greatly different from him, which may have been at the root of his reaction anyway. We had simply grown up in different times.

Avenues were open to me that hadn't been open to him. I could prepare myself to be a man in a different way. In fact, it was absolutely essential that black boys prepare themselves for manhood by taking advantage of every opportunity to educate themselves so that they could compete with girls and boys of whatever race.

Introduction to
Walter Chrysler

Out in Ellis, Kansas, a railroad town in the 1880s, you had to be a tough kid. If you were soft, all the other kids would beat the daylights out of you. So begins Walter Chrysler's description of his childhood in *Life of an American Workman*, the story of the man we identify with the growth of the American automotive industry.

He was a year old when Custer fought his last battle with the Sioux Indians. As a little boy in Kansas, he heard stories of scalpings and kidnappings. But in fact, raids were a thing of the past. With his three older brothers and his robust pioneer mother and father, home was a secure and happy place. Father Henry Chrysler, a railroad engineer, fully expected that Walter and his other sons would work on the railroad one day. He would seat Walter in the cab of his locomotive when on a run, enjoying his son's look of pure joy as the train sped across the prairie, their seat throbbing, hot cinders escaping from the firebox, white smoke snaking across the open sky.

Young Walter loved trains and wanted to know everything about them.

As a restless teenager, Chrysler left Ellis and rode the trains to Cheyenne, Rawlins, and Laramie, Wyoming, and Ogden, Utah, searching for and finding odd jobs, until he had had enough of roaming. In 1919 he took a job in the "young and raw" automobile industry. Within five years, in 1924, he built his first Chrysler car, becoming one of the early giants in the automotive industry.

Walter Chrysler
from Life of an American Workman

For a long time I had been accustomed to making things I wanted when I could not buy them. I had made my first pair of ice skates; later on I made a good shotgun; but in the shops I made, on my own time, a model locomotive.

What I made was a twenty-eight-inch model of the engine my father drove; that was the standard type, which had a four-wheel drive. We had no blueprints then, so I had to do it all myself, laying out my own proportions. Then I took a solid piece of iron and started in to drill and chip and file.

Of course, that engine had to live within my mind so real, so complete that it seemed to have three dimensions there. That, so it seems to me, is what the fault is when someone fails to learn from books. My fingers were like an intake valve through which my mental reservoir was being filled: of course, my eyes and ears were helping in the process, but what I learned with my fingers and my eyes together I seem never to forget.

When the engine model was complete and had many yards of track to run upon, I made it run all around our yard. When its tiny whistle blew, you should have seen my father's mustache widen with his grin of pride.

It must have been about the end of my second year as an apprentice working for the Union Pacific that trouble came. At first I had been paid five cents an hour; for a ten-hour day I got just half of that dollar I had received when I was only a sweeper. But through my second year I got ten cents an hour, and at the time I speak of I was within a few weeks of being entitled to the third-year rate of pay, twelve and a half cents an hour. That was enough money then; I slept and ate at home, and my mother still made most of the clothes I wore. If I worked on the night shift, my mother packed an oblong dinner pail with food enough to fill me up. If I worked days, I went home to lunch—not lunch; that was dinner, then.

Midday, when the shop whistle blew and told Ellis women to get ready for their men, I rushed, with the other soot-and-grease-stained mechanics, to a trough where we washed up. When I had been a sweeper, to fill that long blackened trough with water about ten minutes before noon had been a chore of mine. When all of us had washed our faces, necks, and hands in that trough, the water was a dirty fluid, gray and bubbly.

One day as we began working in the afternoon, the wash trough, neglected by the sweeper, still was filled with dirty water on which floated an iridescent scum. Some of the men were idling there as I resumed the filling of a journal box with grease and wool waste so as to pack this lubricant around the axle end. I was bending over a tub of this grease and wool waste when I got a slimy blow upon the face and ear. Oh, I was mad! A fellow named McGrath had a dripping hand when I looked up: he had, I knew at once, thrown that rag after slopping it in the dirty water in the trough.

I said—well, never mind what I said. The first thing I thought of was going after him. I grabbed deeply into the tub of wool waste and started for him; he ran through a big door, which he slammed behind him. I knew he would not loiter outside long, because he had to run in the direction of the office of the general foreman, Gus Neubert.

I stood before the door, poised as if to throw from second to home plate, and addressing myself over my shoulder to some who mocked my anger, I said, "I'll soak that so-and-so right in the mouth." Then the latch clicked softly, a hinge squeaked, and I flung first one handful and then the other. But it was not McGrath that I splattered in the face: it was Mr. Neubert. He fired me before he had the stuff wiped off.

For some days thereafter I felt as if I had been banished from earth. I was sick; nothing in the world was half so important as my apprenticeship. Maybe my brother Ed helped out by speaking to Mr. Esterbrook, or it may have been my father. At any rate, the master mechanic sent for me. When I stood before his roll-topped desk piled up with papers, he gave me a lecture, which I received contritely.

"That McGrath," I said, "he made me mad. I was working when—"

A vast man, Mr. Esterbrook. When he chuckled, his watch chain, which barely stretched across his vest, moved up and down; I saw it moving then and knew just a trace of hope.

"Next time," he said, "you wait and see who is coming through the door, or catch McGrath outside on your own time. Now, if you apologize to Mr. Neubert, maybe he'll let you come back."

Well, then, with a hangdog manner, I went to Mr. Neubert. I begged his pardon while tears splashed on my chest. He beckoned me to follow him outside the shop where no others could hear him dress me down. For more than half an hour he told me things. At last he said: "This must be a lesson to you. If it ever happens again, I'll fire you sure! And you'll never come back."

When you see a retriever frisking in the ecstasy that comes when you get out your gun, you will know just how I felt when I went back to work. That fright did me a lot of good. From that time on I really settled down to learn, because I knew then just how much I loved mechanics. And now, out in Kansas City, on our payroll, there is the name of a gentleman, a friend of mine, now quite old—the name is Neubert.

Introduction to

Boris Yeltsin

*O*ur *huge country is balanced on a razor's edge, and nobody knows what will happen to it tomorrow.*

These were some of the final words written in Boris Yeltsin's autobiography, titled *Against the Grain.*

Yeltsin has been a feisty fighter for change from the time he was a boy. Both his father and grandfather were tough men, harsh and unbending. This may explain why this Russian leader never caved in to his critics or avoided a challenge. Life was hard in the Soviet Union when Boris was a boy.

Boris Yeltsin rose up the ranks from plant manager, to district representative, to a member of the Party elite in Moscow. But as a result of his criticism of the slow pace of reform under Mikhail Gorbachev, he was forced to resign from his Party position in 1987. He later was elected by the Parliament as Chairman of the Russian Supreme Council. In

1991 he won the first popular election in Russian history to become President of the Russian Federation, a position he held until the end of 1999. During his presidency, he oversaw the dissolution of the Soviet Union and its separation into fifteen independent republics.

Boris Yeltsin

from Against the Grain

We lived in a crowded wooden hut for ten years. Strange as it may seem, the people who lived under those conditions somehow managed to be good, friendly neighbors, especially when one considers that there was no sound insulation. If there was a party in the rooms—a birthday or a wedding—everyone could hear it. There was an old wind-up gramophone with only two or three records, and these were shared by the whole hut; I can still remember one song in particular: "Shchors the Red Commander marches on beneath the standard. . ." which the whole hut used to sing. Conversations, quarrels, rows, secrets, laughter—the whole hut could hear everything, and everyone knew everyone else's business.

Perhaps it is because I can remember to this day how hard our life was then that I so hate those communal huts. Winter was worst of all. There was nowhere to hide from the cold. Since we had no warm clothes, we would huddle up to the nanny goat to keep warm. We children survived on her milk. She was also our salvation throughout the war.

We all earned money on the side. Every summer my mother and I would go out to a nearby collective farm. We would be allotted several acres of meadowland, and we scythed the grass, stacked it, and prepared the hay, half of which went to the collective farm and the other half to us. We would then sell our half and buy bread at exorbitant prices.

That was how my childhood was spent. It was a fairly joyless time. There were never any sweets, delicacies, or anything of that sort; we had only one aim in life—to survive.

Despite these hardships, I always stood out from the other students—especially because of my energy and drive. From first grade on, I was elected class leader, even though I went to several different schools. I did well at my studies and got top marks in my exams. But my behavior was less praiseworthy. In all my years of school I was the ringleader, always devising some mischief. In fifth grade, for instance, I persuaded the whole class to jump out the first-floor window, and when our unpopular teacher came back, the classroom was empty. She immediately went to the watchman at the main entrance, who told her that no one had left the building. We had hidden in a small yard beside the school. When we returned to the classroom we were given a zero for the day. We protested. We said, "Punish us for our bad behavior, but test us on the lesson—we know it." The headmaster arrived, organized a special class, and questioned us for about two hours. We had learned everything by heart, and all of us, even the weak pupils, answered every question correctly. In the end, the zeroes were canceled, although we were given the lowest possible mark for behavior.

I was expelled from school once. It happened at my primary school graduation. About six hundred people were gathered in the assembly hall—parents, teachers, and pupils—in an atmosphere of cheerfulness and elation. Everyone was solemnly handed his or her diploma. Everything was going according to plan, when I suddenly stood up and asked permission to speak. My exam results had been excellent, nothing but top marks in every subject, and for that reason I was allowed up on the stage. Everyone thought that I would simply say a few gracious words. Naturally I had some kind words to say to those teachers who had given us valuable instruction that would help us in our lives and who had developed in us the habits of reading and thinking. But then I declared that our homeroom teacher had no right to teach children because she crippled them mentally and psychologically.

That awful woman might hit you with a heavy ruler, she might stand you in the corner, she might humiliate a boy in front of a girl. She even made us clean her house. Once, the class had to collect food scraps from all over the district to feed her pig. It was endless, and some of the children refused to oblige her, but others submitted.

Briefly I described how she mocked her pupils, destroyed

their self-confidence, and did everything possible to humiliate every one of us—I went for her tooth and nail. There was an uproar. The whole event was ruined.

The next day the school board sent for my father to tell him my diploma was being withdrawn and instead I was to be given a so-called wolf's ticket: a little scrap of white paper that testified to my having completed the required seven years of primary schooling but stated below that I was deprived of the right to acquire a secondary education anywhere in the USSR. My father came home furious and reached for the strap—but at that moment, for the first time, I gripped him by the arm and said, "That's enough. From now on I'm going to educate myself." Never again was I made to stand in the corner all night, and no one ever took the strap to me again.

I refused to accept the decision of the school board and took my case up the education hierarchy: first to the district and then to the city education department. I learned for the first time what a local party committee was. I succeeded in getting a commission of inquiry set up, which investigated the work of that teacher and dismissed her from the school. She got exactly what she deserved, and I got my diploma back, although under the heading "Discipline," the word "unsatisfactory" glared out from the line of otherwise perfect grades.

I decided not to go back to that school and instead entered the eighth grade at Sverdlovsk's Pushkin School, of which I retain the fondest memories. The staff was excellent; and in Angonina Kohonina we had a superb homeroom teacher.

As a boy, I had dreamed of attending an institute of shipbuilding. I had read a number of standard textbooks and tried to understand how ships were built. But gradually I began to be attracted by the profession of civil engineering—no doubt because I had already worked as a building laborer and because my father was in the construction business.

But before I could enter the department of civil engineering at Urals Polytechnic Institute, I had to pass one more test—this one administered by my grandfather. He was over seventy by then, a most impressive man, with a long beard and a quirky, original cast of mind. He said to me, "I won't let you go into the building trade until you have built something with your own hands. You can build me a bathhouse. A small one, in the backyard, complete with a changing room."

We had never had our own bathhouse, though our neighbors did. Circumstances had always prevented us from building one.

My grandfather explained, "You must build it all yourself. My only contribution will be to get the local office of the State Timber Trust to allot you some trees in the forest. From then on you must fell the necessary pine trees, prepare moss for caulking the walls, clean it and dry it; you must carry all the logs from the forest yourself"—it was two miles—"to the place where you're going to build the bathhouse; you must make the foundations and do all the woodworking yourself, all the way up to the roof tree. And I," he said, "will not come anywhere near you." He was a stubborn old man, obstinate as they come, and he never once came within thirty yards of me. Nor did he lift a finger to help me, even though I found the work incredibly hard. When I had finished the bathhouse, my grandfather solemnly announced that I had passed the test and I now had his full permission to enter the department of civil engineering.

Although I hadn't done any special preparation for the entrance exams, because I had been building the bathhouse, I passed them comparatively easily, with two 80s, and 100s for all the other papers. During my first year I plunged into extra-curricular activities. I became president of the sports association, which meant I organized all sporting events. By then I was on the city's volleyball team, and after a year I was playing for Sverdlovsk in the senior league, which competed against the twelve best teams in the country. Throughout my five years at the polytechnic, I played, trained, and traveled all over the Soviet Union with the team. The strain, on top of my studies, was enormous.

After I finished the first year of studies at the institute, I decided to make a journey around the USSR. Until I entered the polytechnic, I had never seen anything of our country; I had never been to the sea and never traveled anywhere far from home. With no money in my pocket and little clothing— sweat pants, tennis shoes, shirt, and straw hat—I left Sverdlovsk. I carried a tiny suitcase of imitation leather, eight by twelve inches in size. It contained one clean shirt, and when I managed to buy food along the way by doing odd jobs, I would put that inside too.

I traveled by train, sometimes on the roofs of passenger cars, sometimes on the open platform at either end of a car. Sometimes I hitched a ride on a truck. More than once I was stopped by the police, who would ask me where I thought I was going. I would say that I was going to see my grandmother in, for instance, Simferopol, in the Crimea. "On which street does she live?" Since I knew every Soviet town had a Lenin Street, I could never be wrong in giving that as my grandmother's address, and they would let me go.

Introduction to

Dan Rather

The final jolt came when I informed my father I intended to major in journalism. That was not a word he could define and it was never clear to him how I thought I could make a living at it. He understood newspapers. But if one was going to college, it was to become a teacher or an engineer or a lawyer.

In his book *The Camera Never Blinks,* Rather describes his struggle to move "up from the ditch," his father's phrase for urging his son to avoid *his* lifetime job of digging ditches for oil pipelines in Texas. Dan's parents, both hard working, hoped that their children would get a better education and have a better life. The dinner table discussion became: What will Danny do with his life? "My mother never wavered in her belief that I absolutely had to go to college. My father," wrote Dan, "wasn't opposed but simply couldn't figure out how they'd pay for it, even if I was given a scholarship." Fresh out of high school Rather entered Sam Houston State Teachers

College, an inexpensive small college, trying to get a sports scholarship. When his journalism professor heard about Rather's attempt to try out as a football player, he told him he was crazy. "You'll get killed!" he said. Instead, his professor helped him get a part-time job as a sports announcer at a local radio station, his first job on radio.

Dan Rather has been a newscaster since 1960 and anchor for the CBS *Evening News* since 1981. He is co-producer of *60 Minutes* and has traveled worldwide, interviewing presidents, statesmen, the rich, the famous, and the infamous. He has received numerous awards for his work.

Dan Rather never dug ditches, but is one of the best at digging up news stories for TV.

Dan Rather

from The Camera Never Blinks

The dream begins, most of the time, with a teacher who believes in you, who tugs and pushes and leads you on to the next plateau, sometimes poking you with a sharp stick called truth.

Mine was named Hugh Cunningham and he taught journalism in 1950 at Sam Houston State Teachers College. With an enrollment sometimes as low as 700 and no pretensions, Sam Houston blended quietly into the red clay and piney woods of East Texas. Traces of the Old South still existed in that part of the state, where cotton, though never king, was about all anyone had. Cotton, lumber and a few scraggly cattle.

With a population of five thousand, Huntsville had grown up around the school, a lean, scenic town with a colorful history. General Sam Houston had built a cabin there and came back to it to die. So the school was named after the liberator of Texas, the hero of San Jacinto and the first elected president of the Lone Star Republic.

For whatever interest it may hold for historians, until the 1920s the official name of the college was the Sam Houston Institute of Teaching. When freshmen started wearing sweatshirts with the school's initials, the state legislature hastily passed an act and renamed it.

How Hugh Cunningham happened to wind up there, with a master's degree from the Missouri School of Journalism, young, with a mind that could light up a room, I do not know. But it was a break for me. Otherwise I would not have lasted in college longer than three weeks and most likely would not have gone on to whatever career I have had. That may be putting too much on one man's conscience, but I owe a debt to Hugh Cunningham.

Actually, my ticket to college was to have been football. Based on my size (I weighed one-fifty), and my talent, which was marginal, there was no reason, other than my own ignorance, for me to think that the gridiron would become my salvation. But I had started as end in my senior year at Reagan High School in Houston and I had shown I could catch a pass. There was nothing to indicate I was a gifted athlete, nothing to feed the hope that it would pay my way through college, except that it was the only hope I had.

So near the end of my last high school year I dropped by the gymnasium to see the coach, a man named Larnar Camp. Football coaches tend to be a major influence on a young man's life. Coach Camp had kept me in school when I wanted to drop out and get a job, the choice people in my neighborhood often faced around the tenth grade.

"I want to start looking for a college," I told him.

"That's fine," he said. Coach Camp was a taciturn man.

"It occurs to me that it might help if I had a letter from you," I replied.

He stared at me for several moments. I thought he hadn't understood what I meant. Finally he just said, "Look, you're not going to play college football. You're not big enough. You're not fast enough. You're not good enough."

There was no misunderstanding what *he* meant and I was absolutely crushed by it. I went home, in a daze, to decide if college was so important after all. Neither of my parents had finished high school. My father, Irvin Rather—known to his friends as Rags—had worked as a pipeliner for twenty years, which meant that he dug ditches for a fair amount of his lifetime. He met my mother, Byrl, at the Travelers' Hotel in Victoria, where she worked as a waitress, fresh off the farm, sending money back home every week to help her family through the Depression.

Mother later passed a high school equivalency test and took a few night classes at a junior college. But basically, they were not people who understood what a college education represented, other than as something a lucky few people strived for, a goal. Their immediate concern was to feed and clothe three kids. I was the oldest, born on the last day of

October, 1931, at Wharton. Then came Don and Patricia, six and eight years younger.

I don't intend for this to sound like another version of Up from Poor. We were not poverty-stricken, but money was always tight. My father felt that if I finished high school that would be achievement enough, as indeed in the 1940s it was. As far back as our heirloom Bibles recorded, no one on either side of our family had ever attended college.

Yet, in a curious way, I developed my passion to become a reporter through my father. That was all I could ever remember wanting to do, to work for a newspaper. I never thought of broadcasting as a career until I was nearly out of college. But radio did intrigue me. As a boy in Houston I listened to the broadcasts of the roller derby at the City Coliseum. Sometimes as I walked to school I would reconstruct in my mind my own roller derby play-by-play. I was, vicariously, the greatest roller derby describer who ever lived.

At home I was surrounded by newspapers. My father was an impulse subscriber, a voracious reader, and a man of sudden angers who would leap from his chair and cancel whichever paper had offended him. We went through every newspaper in town, the *Post*, the *Chronicle*, and the *Press*, which was part of the Scripps-Howard chain and known locally for its muckraking policies. There was a constant harangue about newspapers in our house. My father would read something in the *Press* that riled him and he would shout, "Mother, cancel the *Press*. We're through with that paper forever. I don't want to ever see it in here again."

At one point we were down to the *Christian Science Monitor* and the St. Louis *Post-Dispatch*, which arrived in the mail, usually a week late.

Out of that cycle, somehow, grew my interest in the news, how it was gathered and reported and in what form it reached our home. I had always written for the school papers, usually on sports, and in the summer of 1948 had worked at the *Press* as a gofer. That, of course, was just below a copyboy. I'd go for coffee or cigars or egg rolls, or whatever the reporters needed.

I was still determined to get to college and my mother, bless her, was adamant that I should make the attempt. I considered myself fairly street-smart. I had been to sea briefly one summer, at sixteen, worked on an oil rig, and dug pipeline ditches. But no money had been set aside for my schooling. It was that way with most families.

So I picked out the nearest small school with a full, four-year enrollment, and that happened to be Sam Houston State, seventy-five miles northeast of Houston. I knew nothing else about it, but I hitchhiked to Huntsville and asked around for the football coach. I found him in the basketball gym, a little crackerbox the students used to call the Tarpaper Tabernacle. He was watching a game, his head swiveling from side to side, and the entire time I talked to him he never once looked me in the eye.

I said, "Coach, I'm Dan Rather. I'm from Houston, Reagan

High School, and I'm a football player."

He said, "Uh-huh," and in a very fishlike way he shook my hand.

This meeting was my introduction to Puny Wilson, who had been a great football player at Texas A&M in the days when the All-America selectors did their picking from the Ivy League. According to local legend, Puny Wilson also had the distinction of being the only football coach in the nation who actually, honestly, had a degree in basket weaving.

When he was in college, peach growing was the rage in East Texas towns eager for new income. The peach crops created a demand for baskets in which to ship the fruit. So the Agricultural and Mechanical College of Texas offered an undergraduate certificate in basket weaving, and Coach Puny had one.

He was a disillusioned man long before that day in 1950 when I approached him in the gym. Fourteen straight losing seasons will do that to a coach.

My conversation with him was painful, punctuated by long silences. I explained to him that I would graduate at midterm and could enroll for the next semester, which was to begin the fifteenth of February.

He said, "Well, spring training starts March sixth and I'd be glad to have you come out."

That was all I needed to hear. It was an invitation to try out for the team and, in my mind, that was tantamount to a scholarship. I was ecstatic as I hitchhiked the seventy-five miles to Houston. When I told my mother the news, she was jubilant. Then my dad came home and he thought it was madness. One, there was no money to cover my living expenses. Two, my football tryout did not sound like a very solid arrangement to him. And, three, there was a lapse of maybe three weeks between the start of classes and spring training.

The final jolt came when I informed my father I intended to major in journalism. That was not a word he could define and it was never clear to him how I thought I could make a living at it. He understood newspapers. But if one was going to college, it was to become a teacher or an engineer or a lawyer.

The days passed very quickly, and what my mother instinctively knew was that if I didn't go off to school immediately, I would never get there. She was simply very determined about it. She had never been on a university campus, but her feeling was that once I enrolled something would work out.

In February 1950, Mother took me to Huntsville on the Greyhound bus. We had a car, a 1938 Oldsmobile, but there was some doubt as to whether it would hold together, so we rode the bus. In my lifetime I have not made many more exciting trips than that one. We went first to the office of the dean of men, where I mentioned, proudly, that I was a candidate for the football team.

The dean replied that he didn't know anything about that, but registration ended that week and I needed $25 to enroll and $15 for student fees. My mother had brought along two $25 U.S. Saving Bonds—bought during the war and not yet worth their full value—and while I waited in the dean's office she went into town and cashed them.

There was just enough money to cover all the fees, and when I was enrolled I could only guess what my mother felt. I don't know if anyone who didn't live or grow up during the war will understand what my mother had done. But a family paid $18.75 for a savings bond and waited ten years for it to mature and pay back $25. You cashed one only in an emergency.

Again, this isn't meant as Humble Beginnings nostalgia. That was simply the way it was. Next I found a boardinghouse a block from the campus and the manager agreed to give me a month's credit.

I had a great sense of satisfaction about the whole process. Really, I was very little different from the farmers' sons and daughters who were enrolling that day, the youngsters who had been valedictorians in Roans Prairie and Sundown and North Zulch, who carried whatever they owned in cardboard boxes wrapped with rope. Or the workmen's kids from Beaumont and Dallas and Houston, who lacked the money or the grades to get into the bigger universities. I felt at home, walking the grounds in my blue jeans, open-neck white shirt, and tennis shoes.

Later, when I signed up for classes, I paid my first visit to the young journalism professor, Hugh Cunningham. He had started the department and only had five or six students enrolled. That suited him fine. His idea was to work with a small number of young people and turn out a handcrafted product.

Where journalism was concerned he had a jealous nature. "Why are you here?" he demanded. "Do you know why you want to major in journalism?"

I said, "It's the only thing I've ever wanted to do."

He said, "What makes you think you can do it?"

I kind of bristled. "Well, I *know* I can."

With that reply, he barked out a half dozen facts and he had me sit down and write a news story for him. Now that I think about it, I was in the odd position of having to try out for the journalism department even before the football team.

From that moment Cunningham took me under his wing. When he heard about my football plans, he threw up his hands.

"That's crazy," he said. "You don't want to be a football player. You'll get killed."

"There's no other way I can stay in school," I said. "This way I'll get a scholarship."

He laughed out loud. But he didn't push me about it. Possibly he knew it would do no good. Sometimes we ought not to be talked out of our mistakes. But I had to survive the next three weeks before the football practices started, and during that time Cunningham literally fed me out of his own pocket. In the meantime he kept lining up part-time jobs for me. I became a correspondent for the local Huntsville *Item*, which neither then nor now would be mistaken for one of America's distinguished newspapers. I was to string for the wire services—calling in basketball scores, mostly—and I also received ten dollars a month for cranking out publicity about the college. He had put together a package that would allow me at least to tread water.

In addition, I held a series of odd jobs, none of which lasted very long: I waited tables, pumped gas, worked at the Zesto Tastee-Freeze stand. It was a dollar here and a dollar there and then it was time to report for football. Just as Cunningham had warned, I damned near got killed. To begin with, we had played two-platoon football in high school and I knew nothing about defense. Beyond that I lacked speed and couldn't block.

As if my other handicaps were not enough, Puny Wilson had a fearful prejudice toward city boys. He was a big, rawboned ol' country boy himself and he typed me—this was laughable—as just another pampered, big-city dude. His idea of a gut check, of putting a youngster to the test, was to stick the candidate at defensive end and run one power sweep after another in his direction. In the first two weeks of practice I did not distinguish myself. Cunningham used to drop by the practice field, a cow pasture really, and he would stand there, shake his head, and cover his eyes when the herd rumbled over my body.

Finally it dawned on me that Coach Puny was trying to make me quit. One afternoon as I limped toward the showers he ambled over, dressed as usual in a T-shirt, football pants, and army surplus boots. He splattered a missile of tobacco juice amid the sand and cockleburs, rubbed the stubble of his beard, then put his arm around me. It was the first human gesture he had shown me.

"Son," he said, "I watched ya out thar the whole time t'day. And I wanna tell ya sumptun' I hope'll stay with ya the rest of your life. You're little." Pause. "And you're *yellow*!"

Well, I set about trying to prove he had at least the last part of it wrong. The proof was to be that I wouldn't quit. I played day after day, getting my bones smashed. Finally I went to see him and asked about my scholarship. Coach Puny was a tough, no-nonsense man, about fifty, and this time he didn't try to belittle me. I think he sensed that I really wanted to stay in school and that I needed help. For all I know, Cunningham may have put the fix in. Anyway, Puny said, "There's no way you can get a scholarship. But if you want to come back out in the fall, practice starts August fifteenth." (This was the same routine we had gone through before, but I accepted it, again, as an invitation.)

But I realized he had a heart when he told me I could drop around to the Bearcat Den—that was where they fed the football team—and take my meals on weekends. Coach Puny knew the boardinghouse, where I was eating on credit, closed its kitchen on the weekend.

I struggled through that spring and, in spite of everything, the odd jobs and the strange meal arrangements, Hugh Cunningham managed to capture and hold my attention. He was about five nine, slight, with dark hair combed straight back. An intensity poured out of him like water from a fire hose.

His idea of teaching journalism was to get you away from the classroom. He didn't believe the reporter's craft could be taught in school, and when he did, it was only because the state required it. The college had to have a curriculum. There had to be a Journalism 101. But Hugh Cunningham didn't really give a damn about any of that. He wanted us out in the field. "Write stories," he kept hammering at us. "Go interview the college horticulturist. Go downtown. Hang around the courthouse. Ride with the police. I don't want to see you the rest of the afternoon."

I learned long ago that the term *a good teacher* is redundant, while the phrase *a bad teacher* is a contradiction in terms. Rare is the teacher who fully understands what a tremendous difference he or she can make, but Cunningham was one of them. He picked the courses his students needed to get a degree, and he set their standards. Often he lectured me: "Coming out of a school this size, with no reputation at all, your only chance is to make virtually straight A's."

That admonition I took to heart. I studied as hard as I could without actually feeling pain. Before breakfast, in the afternoons and at night I worked at money-paying jobs. Classes were crammed into the morning hours. Homework was done in snatches of time during the day and after midnight. In between and all about was the school paper. With

Cunningham and Cecil Tuck, we put out the *Houstonian* twice a week. Tuck was another of Cunningham's prize students. He eventually went to Hollywood and has done well writing for television. He helped to discover and promote Glen Campbell, among others. Cecil was in much the same financial shape as I was, maybe worse. He stayed in school that semester by writing bad checks and then scrambling to cover them. Truth to tell, we often covered for one another with criss-crossing hot checks. We always paid our bills, but some semesters it took longer than others.

Meanwhile, Cunningham kept preaching experience to us, that you learned to write by writing. Cecil and I would compose stories and mail them to the Houston *Post*. Heaven knows, most of the time no response came and none was really expected. We would just send them off into this great vacuum. We'd do a feature story on a football player, or a teacher, or some campus character. Once, we sent out a piece on the lady who maintained Sam Houston's home. That was the big bone. The story was published and we were very proud. (You could get that feature printed almost every year. Even today. There is something about Sam Houston still having a housekeeper that seems to impress big city editors.)

Cecil was a major presence at the college. He was sloppy and fun and we hit it off from the beginning. He came from a sawmill town near Jasper and for that place, and for those times, he was an authentic free spirit. I believe he still holds the Lone Star Conference record for gin consumed by a third-string linebacker. He would occasionally show up for football practice under the influence, as they say, and he did not take many things seriously, including Cunningham.

Hugh was always torn. He knew he was a gifted teacher, knew how much of himself he was putting into us. But at the same time he wanted to be on the cutting edge of journalism. He was always taking summer jobs at newspapers like the Atlanta *Constitution*. He saw things in us and tried to express them in the way a father would, but he finally gave up trying to convince Cecil.

He couldn't talk to Tuck the way he could to me. Cecil would fall asleep or say, "Aw, come off that shit." So Cunningham would say to me, with a wrenching earnestness, "You can do it, Dan. You can go all the way." Keep in mind that for Hugh Cunningham, getting a job with the Houston *Post* was going all the way. A byline in the Houston *Chronicle* would have given him raptures. That was going all the way.

Cecil Tuck was country down to his toes. I never knew how or why he wanted to be a reporter. But we came along at the same time, and for the next three and a half years Cunningham tutored and pushed us. It was a fine relationship. I cannot imagine any student, anywhere, having a more meaningful one.

All that summer of my freshman year my major concern was winning a football scholarship in the fall of 1950. I still saw no way to stay in school without it. I landed a job during the summer working on a pipeline gang, digging ditches, as my father had done for so many years. I was able to save almost two hundred dollars and that relieved some of the pressure.

Still, it wasn't enough to get me through the school year. The money I had earned only meant that I could pay my bill at the boardinghouse and not mooch off Cunningham. So when football practice started in the fall I was there, drawing a uniform. The coaches looked at me with a weary respect. I was like a bastard cat you keep throwing off the end of the dock, and by the time you drive home he's waiting on the doorstep. But I stuck it out, long after all the others who didn't have scholarships had quit, and one or two more had given theirs back.

Before the first game I went to Coach Puny again and asked him where I stood. I think he may have been getting used to me. He still wouldn't give me a scholarship, he said, but I could suit out for the games if I wanted. I believe part of him wanted me to make it. We had a fine passer that year named Cotton Gottlob, and he knew I could catch the ball. There was always the possibility that the eight ends ahead of me might get hurt.

I worked out every day, letting the power sweep roll over me in waves, and I suited out for the first three games. Finally, in a fit of conscience, Coach Puny Wilson called me in and said, "Son, take my advice—give it up. It's useless for you." And that was it. I can remember walking out of his office and into the rain. Tears streamed down my face. It was one of the few times in my life I can remember crying.

My pride was involved. I had put so much of myself,

emotionally, into it. And there was the feeling that I wouldn't last through the school year. All of that just came down on me.

Hugh Cunningham picked me right up. "It's the best thing that ever happened to you," he said. "You'd have wound up coaching or crippled or both. You don't know how lucky you are."

The next thing I knew he had obtained a job for me at the radio station in Huntsville, KSAM. It was Kay Sam to all who knew the station, what was known in the trade as a teakettle. Kay Sam had an operating power of 250 watts, the lowest allowed by the FCC. It was a three-room shack with a tower in the back, an oversized outhouse with an antenna sticking out the top. Our signal did not even carry to the city limits of Huntsville. We used to sell advertising to merchants over in Madisonville, fifteen miles away, and nobody in Madisonville could hear the station after six o'clock.

Kay Sam was basic, good ol' boy radio. We used to sell time on the pitch of a dollar a holler—the idea being that advertising spots cost a dollar each—but we often cut the price to forty cents.

The station was owned and managed by a Baptist minister known as Pastor Lott, Ted Lott. He was a journalist at heart. He loved the stories, the newscasting. He took a genuine liking to me, but I also filled a need for the station. He wanted to know if I had ever done any play-by-play of football games, and I said no, but I was sure I could.

He said, "Well, let me hear you. Go ahead, do some."

So I sat there and made up a game in my head, using the players from Sam Houston and a mythical opposing team. Altogether I did five or six minutes, and it wasn't difficult. It was not unlike the times I had invented a broadcast of the roller derby on the way to school or other occasions when I would amuse myself with the play-by-play of an imaginary football game in which I would be the hero with two seconds left on the clock.

When I walked out of the station, Cunningham was gleeful. "Now that does it," he said. "If you really do a job for him, that's going to keep you in school and you'll have no more worries."

SPORTS

Now bid me run,
And I will strive with things impossible,
Yea, get the better of them.
—William Shakespeare, from *Julius Caesar*

Introduction to

Sammy Sosa

The Dominican Republic has been one of the most likely places to find new, talented baseball players in recent times. In the barrios and small towns, in vacant lots and dirt fields where young boys play ball, scouts come looking for new talent. It was there that fourteen-year-old Sammy Sosa was first discovered batting balls made of corn husks with a wooden broomstick. He had quit school to help his impoverished parents by shining shoes and washing automobiles for a pittance. There was little time for sports but whenever he could, he played ball with his brother and friends.

San Pedro is a working town filled with people and factories. Later, I took a job in one of those factories—a job that changed my life.

Every day Sammy and his brother, Juan, shined the shoes of a successful businessman named William Chase, an American from Bristol, Maine, who offered Sammy and Juan jobs in his shoe factory after seeing how hard they worked. Bill Chase became a mentor and friend. He and his wife provided the two skinny boys with extra food, and when Sammy was twelve, bought him his first bike. But the gift that made the most difference in his young life was his first baseball glove.

Sammy Sosa's career had many ups and downs during his first nine seasons as a professional. Sometimes he was called "Sammy So-So," a player who didn't score well, who seemed too overconfident and proud—that is, until 1996, when Sosa was leading the National League in home runs at the all-star break. Still, Sosa didn't achieve enough respect to make the team as a reserve. It wasn't until the 1998 season and again in 1999 that Sosa became a superstar by hitting sixty-three home runs in one season—and 129 home runs in two seasons. It has been said that before Sammy Sosa, baseball fans in this country—black and white—had never given a foreign-born athlete as much admiration and affection as he was given after matching the record of Mark McGwire.

Sammy Sosa

from Sosa: An Autobiography

In my country small boys begin playing baseball not long after they learn to walk. In every town and village in any part of the island, you'll see them playing pickup games in the streets, in alleys, in parks, and in open fields. When I was a boy, baseball was the only sport in the Dominican Republic. It's still our national game. The people here follow it the year-round. From April to October, Dominicans are glued to their television sets and scan the box scores of the major-league baseball season, just as Americans do.

And from November to February, the whole island closely follows the Dominican Winter League, whose teams are filled mostly with Dominican major leaguers who use the winter to hone their skills.

Also in February is the Caribbean World Series, a tournament where our league champions compete against the league champions from Puerto Rico, Venezuela, and Mexico.

Each country takes turns hosting the tournament, and it's always a huge source of pride when we win—which we have done many times. During those games Dominican flags are everywhere, and my people show their national pride and deep love for the game of baseball. Along with Dominican Independence Day, which is February 27, Caribbean Series time is always a special series of days for my country.

There is a passion for baseball in my country that I love. People here build lifelong allegiances to local teams—Estrellas Orientales, Licey, Escogido, Aguilas, and so on—just as Americans do for the Yankees, Mets, Dodgers, or Cubs. And for young people there are dozens of little-league and amateur leagues in every region of the Dominican Republic.

Boys practice for those leagues all week long and play intense games on the weekends. It's no wonder there are so many Dominican players in the big leagues today because, for our young boys, baseball is everything. Everybody here knows that big-league teams have scouts all over the island, just as they know there is an even bigger network of people who follow even the most remote amateur-league games in the hope of seeing a flash of talent that they can then recommend to a scout.

But despite this history, which goes back many years, I didn't play any organized baseball as a young boy. I didn't have the love for the game back then, which made me the exception to the rule. Our financial situation was so critical I simply didn't have the time to do much else besides work and earn money.

When I did play baseball, I played on the street, using balled-up rags for baseballs and sticks for bats. That's a lot different from working with coaches and drilling in fundamentals. In my life, in my preteen years, coaches and ball games complete with uniforms were something for other kids.

I didn't have any plans to play organized baseball. Though Bill Chase had been nice enough to give me my first real baseball glove, I wanted to be an athlete of another kind—a professional fighter.

I wanted to be like Sugar Ray Leonard, Tommy Hearns, and Marvin Hagler. In the early 1980s, those fighters were the kings of boxing, and I loved the way they fought. I had fought a lot in the streets when I was a kid, defending myself and proving to the other kids that I was tough. So already having the inclination, I found out San Pedro had a boxing school soon after we moved there. Soon I was attending, squeezing training sessions in between my work hours at Bill Chase's shoe factory.

I used to get up early in the morning and do road work. I would spar, and hit the speed bag and the heavy bag. I trained hard for months. There haven't been many well-known fighters from the Dominican Republic, but that didn't worry me. The truth is, I wanted to be a champion boxer.

In our family it was my brother Luis who loved baseball, who played the game and knew the game. It was his passion, and he tried to get me interested, but I had my own plans. And as I had done since I was a small child, I kept them to myself.

Luis knew what I was doing, but I hadn't discussed my goal of a boxing career with my mother. Maybe I knew in my heart that she wouldn't approve. So I told myself I would tell her later—much later.

It went on this way for almost a year. In a way, I was already living like an adult. I had quit school, was working long hours, and was spending my time on my goals. And I knew how to fight. I was good at it, even though my fans probably wouldn't have recognized me back then. Like a lot of Dominican kids of my background, I was very thin and hadn't come close to developing physically. All I had was a lot of desire.

I thought I had what it took to be a fighter, but, fortunately for me, the people who loved me the most had other ideas. My mother remembers it like it was yesterday.

Mireya Sosa:

One day Luis came up to me and said, "Mom, did you know that Sammy is practicing to be a boxer?"

I thought, "No. I don't want my son to be a fighter." I was terribly worried, but I knew, because Sammy was such a serious boy, that I had to find the right way to tell him. Luis said, "Mom, I don't want Sammy to think that I'm betraying a confidence."

And I reassured Luis that I would find the right way. For the next two weeks that's all I thought about, and I tried to find the words. Sammy had always been a good and obedient boy, but I still worried about saying the right thing. Then, one day, we were alone together, and I decided it was time. I said, "Son, come sit down here, I want to talk to you."

"Sí, Mama."

"Son, I've come to know that you are boxing, and I want to ask you to please stop. With all my heart I'm asking you to give it up. Please don't do it anymore."

"Why, Mom?"

"Son, hear me when I say this. Do you think that if you became a boxer that I could sit and watch you strike someone else or see someone hit you?"

"Mom, that would be no big deal."

"Son, it is a big deal. Do you know what it would be for a mother to see her own son getting hit? It would kill me to see that. No, son, please don't do this. Please give this up." At that moment Sammy didn't say anything. I hoped he had listened to what I said because it hurt my heart to think of him exchanging punches with someone else.

Thank God, after some time passed, he gave me the wonderful news. "Mom," he announced, "I quit boxing."

"Oh, thank God, son. Thank God."

But he had another surprise for me. Sammy loves giving me surprises, as he did on Mother's Day when he was a boy. That he wanted to tell me his plans made me feel at ease because I knew whatever it was would be better than his interest in boxing—which he had tried to keep from me. To my surprise, he told me he wanted to play baseball.

"You see, son! That's an idea I like! Baseball is a good thing for you to do because the only way you could get hurt is through bad luck, not because someone was trying to hurt you." I gave him my blessing, and from then on my son was a baseball player.

Sammy:

I could never do something like boxing if my mother was so opposed to it. I trusted her and valued her opinion, so I decided it wasn't for me. It was then that my brother Luis got me into baseball and set me on the path that I follow to this day.

I was able to get Bill Chase's permission to play ball a couple of days a week on work time. Once that happened, I started practicing baseball all the time, but it was still difficult for me because I had a lot of responsibility as well. At a certain point, I knew I needed to devote more time to baseball. So I talked to Bill Chase about it, and he agreed to hire my younger brother so our family wouldn't lose any income and I could continue to play ball.

When Bill Chase gave me his permission, my life became all about baseball. We were living in a two-room house near an abandoned hospital by this point, better than what we had known in Santo Domingo but still very humble. Like our other places, the house had dirt floors and one room that was cordoned off into sleeping quarters with bed sheets that my mother hung on ropes.

Every morning, I would get up at 6:00 A.M. and go to

practice. I would run a lot and do anything I could to improve. I grew to love the game, but make no mistake: My dream was to help my mother.

It was while working at baseball that I realized I had talent. With my brother Luis, we would play in different barrios of San Pedro, with me learning something new with each game. Back then I always wore cut-off jeans, and I would practice on my street by hitting dried husks of maize again and again.

I would tell my friends that I was going to be a big-league ballplayer and they would say, "You're crazy. You're never going to amount to anything." But I never paid them any attention because I knew I had the dedication that set me apart from the others. By this point I had made up my mind what I was going to do with my life. I stayed out of trouble and remained very close to my mother and family. For me there weren't any days off. I worked at baseball every day.

And then, when he thought I was ready, Luis took me to see Hector Peguero, who had a reputation around San Pedro for knowing a lot about baseball. Hector ran a team in a local amateur league, and my brother knew he could help me.

Hector and I are still friends to this day, and I drive four hours, round-trip from my home in Santo Domingo, to practice with him and some other friends during the off-season. Sometimes, he still tells me when he sees something he doesn't like in my swing. And we still sometimes talk about that first day he saw me.

Hector Peguero:

Luis Sosa had played on a team that I ran, and so we knew each other. And one day, he initiated a conversation with me. He said, "Hector, I have a kid with big hands who I want you to look at."

So he brought Sammy to the park, and the first thing I noticed was that he was strong. But he was also what we call here kind of a "lobo," which means kind of wild and raw. He didn't have much experience. I said, "Let's put him out on the field and see what he can do."

And so he started practicing with some other kids. He was playing in the outfield and then I saw him throw. Wow! He had a really strong arm.

Soon, I had gotten him onto my team in our league in San Pedro. We played with game uniforms, but his uniform didn't fit—he was a little bigger than the other kids on his team. So we moved him up to play against the bigger kids. And I swear, every time someone tried to run from second to home against him he would throw him out. One time the manager of another team accused Sammy of being a ringer. He claimed that Sammy was older than he really was. I said, "No, he's only fourteen."

Introduction to

Lance Armstrong

My mother was seventeen when she had me, and from day one everyone told her we wouldn't amount to anything, but she believed differently, and she raised me with an unbending rule: "Make every obstacle an opportunity." And that's what we did.

Lance Armstrong, one of America's great athletes, never knew his father; nor did he care to. His relationship with his mother and her family was all that mattered.

Lance grew up in a suburb of Dallas, Texas, where his mother worked part-time for Kentucky Fried Chicken and a local grocery store.

During elementary school, his fifth-grade class held a distance running race. Although he'd never tried running, he told his mother the night before the race, "I'm going to be a champ" . . . and won.

This same determination got him through a severe bout with cancer and brain surgery. He was only twenty-five. Given only a 40 percent chance of survival (which was optimistic, according to some doctors), Lance Armstrong proved not only to himself but to the rest of the world that grueling persistence and a will to live sometimes pays off. It paid off again when he competed in his sport, cycling.

After a long three-year course of treatment, Armstrong began to train once more for one of Europe's most difficult bike races, the Tour de France.

"I was the first American riding for an American team, on an American bike, ever to lead the Tour de France," he said. As of this publication, he has won four consecutive Tour de France races, 1999-2002. His best-selling autobiography is compelling, inspirational, one of the best descriptions of overcoming the odds. "It's not (just) about the bike . . . it's about more than sports, it's about hope and a chance at a new life." Here is some of his story about starting over.

Lance Armstrong
from It's Not About the Bike

We lived in a dreary one-bedroom apartment in Oak Cliff, a suburb of Dallas, while my mother worked part-time and finished school. It was one of those neighborhoods with shirts flapping on clotheslines and a Kentucky Fried on the corner. My mother worked at the Kentucky Fried, taking orders in her pink-striped uniform, and she also punched the cash register at the Kroger's grocery store across the street. Later she got a temporary job at the post office sorting dead letters, and another one as a file clerk, and she did all of this while she was trying to study and to take care of me. She made $400 a month, and her rent was $200, and my day-care was $25 a week. But she gave me everything I needed, and a few things more. She had a way of creating small luxuries.

When I was small, she would take me to the local 7-Eleven and buy a Slurpee, and feed it to me through the straw. She would pull some up in the straw, and I would tilt my head back, and she would let the cool, sweet, icy drink stream into my mouth. She tried to spoil me with a 50-cent drink.

Every night she read a book to me. Even though I was just an infant, too young to understand a word, she would hold me and read. She was never too tired for that. "I can't wait until you can read to *me*," she would say. No wonder I was reciting verses by the age of two. I did everything fast. I walked at nine months.

Eventually, my mother got a job as a secretary for $12,000 a year, which allowed her to move us into a nicer apartment north of Dallas in a suburb called Richardson. She later got a job at a telecommunications company, Ericsson, and she has worked her way up the ladder. She's no longer a secretary, she's an account manager, and what's more, she got her real-estate license on the side. That right there tells you everything you need to know about her. She's sharp as a tack, and she'll outwork anybody. She also happens to look young enough to be my sister.

After Oak Cliff, the suburbs seemed like heaven to her. North Dallas stretches out practically to the Oklahoma border in an unbroken chain of suburban communities, each one exactly like the last. Tract homes and malls overrun miles of flat brown Texas landscape. But there are good schools and lots of open fields for kids to play in.

Across the street from our apartment there was a little store called the Richardson Bike Mart at one end of a strip mall. The owner was a small, well-built guy with overly bright eyes named Jim Hoyt. Jim liked to sponsor bike racers out of his store, and he was always looking to get kids started in the sport. One morning a week my mother would take me to a local shop for fresh, hot doughnuts and we would pass by the bike store. Jim knew she struggled to get by, but he noticed that she was always well turned out, and I was neat and well cared for. He took an interest in us, and gave her a deal on my first serious bike. It was a Schwinn Mag Scrambler, which I got when I was about seven. It was an ugly brown, with yellow wheels, but I loved it. Why does any kid love a bike? It's liberation and independence, your first set of wheels. A bike is freedom to roam, without rules and without adults.

There was one thing my mother gave me that I didn't particularly want—a stepfather. When I was three, my mother remarried, to a guy named Terry Armstrong. Terry was a small man with a large mustache and a habit of acting more successful than he really was. He sold food to grocery stores and he was every cliché of a traveling salesman, but he brought home a second paycheck and helped with the bills. Meanwhile, my mother was getting raises at her job, and she bought us a home in Plano, one of the more upscale suburbs.

I was a small boy when Terry legally adopted me and made my name Armstrong, and I don't remember being happy or unhappy about it, either way. All I know is that the DNA donor, Gunderson, gave up his legal rights to me. In order for the adoption to go through, Gunderson had to allow it, to agree to it. He picked up a pen and signed the papers.

Terry Armstrong was a Christian, and he came from a family

who had a tendency to tell my mother how to raise me. But, for all of his proselytizing, Terry had a bad temper, and he used to whip me, for silly things. Kid things, like being messy.

Once, I left a drawer open in my bedroom, with a sock hanging out. Terry got out his old fraternity paddle. It was a thick, solid wood paddle, and frankly, in my opinion nothing like that should be used on a small boy. He turned me over and spanked me with it.

The paddle was his preferred method of discipline. If I came home late, out would come the paddle. *Whack*. If I smarted off, I got the paddle. *Whack*. It didn't hurt just physically, but also emotionally. So I didn't like Terry Armstrong. I thought he was an angry testosterone geek, and as a result, my early impression of organized religion was that it was for hypocrites.

Athletes don't have much use for poking around in their childhoods, because introspection doesn't get you anywhere in a race. You don't want to think about your adolescent resentments when you're trying to make a 6,500-foot climb with a cadre of Italians and Spaniards on your wheel. You need a dumb focus. But that said, it's all stoked down in there, fuel for the fire. "Make every negative into a positive," as my mother says. Nothing goes to waste, you put it all to use, the old wounds and long-ago slights become the stuff of competitive energy. But back then I was just a kid with about four chips on his shoulder, thinking, *Maybe if I ride my bike on this road long enough it will take me out of here.*

Plano had its effect on me, too. It was the quintessential

American suburb, with strip malls, perfect grid streets, and faux-antebellum country clubs in between empty brown wasted fields. It was populated by guys in golf shirts and Sansabelt pants, and women in bright, fake gold jewelry, and alienated teenagers. Nothing there was old, nothing real. To me, there was something soul-deadened about the place, which may be why it had one of the worst heroin problems in the country, as well as an unusually large number of teen suicides. It's home to Plano East High School, one of the largest and most football-crazed high schools in the state, a modern structure that looks more like a government agency, with a set of doors the size of loading docks. That's where I went to school.

In Plano, Texas, if you weren't a football player you didn't exist, and if you weren't upper middle class, you might as well not exist either. My mother was a secretary, so I tried to play football. But I had no coordination. When it came to anything that involved moving from side to side, or hand-eye coordination—when it came to anything involving a ball, in fact—I was no good.

I was determined to find something I could succeed at. When I was in fifth grade, my elementary school held a distance-running race. I told my mother the night before the race, "I'm going to be a champ." She just looked at me, and then she went into her things and dug out a 1972 silver dollar. "This is a good-luck coin," she said. "Now remember, all you have to do is beat that clock." I won the race.

A few months later, I joined the local swim club. At first it was another way to seek acceptance with the other kids in the suburbs, who all swam laps at Los Rios Country Club, where their parents were members. On the first day of swim practice, I was so inept that I was put with the seven-year-olds. I looked around, and saw the younger sister of one of my friends. It was embarrassing. I went from not being any good at football to not being any good at *swimming*.

But I tried. If I had to swim with the little kids to learn technique, then that's what I was willing to do. My mother gets emotional to this day when she remembers how I leaped headfirst into the water and flailed up and down the length of the pool, as if I was trying to splash all the water out of it. "You tried so *hard*," she says. I didn't swim in the worst group for long.

Swimming is a demanding sport for a twelve-year-old, and the City of Plano Swim Club was particularly intense. I swam for a man named Chris MacCurdy, who remains one of the best coaches I ever worked with. Within a year, Chris transformed me; I was fourth in the state in the 1,500-meter freestyle. He trained our team seriously: we had workouts every morning from 5:30 to 7:00. Once I got a little older I began to ride my bike to practice, ten miles through the semi-dark early-morning streets. I would swim 4,000 meters of laps before school and go back for another two-hour workout in the afternoon—another 6,000 meters. That was six miles a day in the water, plus a 20-mile bike ride. My mother let me do it for two reasons: she didn't have the option of driving me herself because she worked, and she knew that I needed to channel my temperament.

One afternoon when I was about thirteen and hanging around the Richardson Bike Mart, I saw a flyer for a competition called IronKids. It was a junior triathlon, an event that combined biking, swimming, and running. I had never heard of a triathlon before—but it was all of the things I was good at, so I signed up. My mother took me to a shop and bought me a triathlon outfit, which basically consisted of crosstraining shorts and a shirt made out of a hybrid fast-drying material, so I could wear it through each phase of the event, without changing. We got my first racing bike then, too. It was a Mercier, a slim, elegant road bike.

I won, and I won by a lot, without even training for it. Not long afterward, there was another triathlon, in Houston. I won that, too. When I came back from Houston, I was full of self-confidence. I was a top junior at swimming, but I had never been the absolute best at it. I was better at triathlons than any kid in Plano, and any kid in the whole state, for that matter. I liked the feeling.

What makes a great endurance athlete is the ability to absorb potential embarrassment, and to suffer without complaint. I was discovering that if it was a matter of gritting my teeth, not caring how it looked, and outlasting everybody else, I won. It didn't seem to matter what the sport was—in a straight-ahead, long-distance race, I could beat anybody.

If it was a suffer-fest, I was good at it.

Introduction to

Jackie Joyner-Kersee

The book *A Kind of Grace* is the autobiography of the woman called the world's greatest female athlete. For the young Jackie Joyner, "all arms and legs," as she described herself as a ten-year-old, this title would have seemed only a joke. She was born to two teenage parents—her mother was eighteen, her father sixteen. They were kids raising kids. Jackie was the second of four children, two born within a year of each other. Her father, handsome and athletic, measuring six feet, two inches tall, 190 pounds, was still in high school when he married Mary, her mother. After he graduated and found work, with a family of four little children to support, there were times when all they had for dinner were peanut butter sandwiches.

The six of them moved in with Jackie's great-grandmother in her small six-room house in East St. Louis, Illinois. When the furnace broke down in wintertime, a frequent occurrence, the family lived in the kitchen heated by the kitchen stove. Leaving the oven on day and night wasn't safe, "but it was either that or freeze. At night the heated kitchen floor was our mattress," wrote Kersee.

Looking back, she wrote, the most significant event of her childhood was the building of a community center nearby featuring a library, arts and crafts, dancing, and sports. "The Center revealed a whole new world to me, teaching me things I wouldn't have learned otherwise . . . I was a human sponge, soaking up as much as I could," said Kersee, and this included basketball, cheerleading, and modern dance. Her dance teacher, Mr. Wilson, was an admirer of the internationally renowned dancer and choreographer Katherine Dunham, one of the first African-Americans to have her own dance company. When she was in St. Louis, she would visit the Saturday dance classes and talk to the students. She became a role model for some, and now Jackie's question was, "Could I be a Broadway dancer?" Wilson told Jackie that she had talent, and that "your legs are long and powerful. That's what a good dancer needs."

But the tragic death of her teacher and a sudden twist of fate changed how she used her gift of long powerful legs, and newfound talents led ten-year-old Jackie Joyner to her lifelong career and worldwide fame.

In 1991 Jackie Joyner-Kersee was forced to withdraw from an international race after pulling a hamstring in her leg. Then in 1995 recurring asthma attacks meant she would have to wear a breathing mask during a U.S. championship event. Her husband, who was also her coach, finally insisted that she face the reality of too much risk-taking. She had achieved all that she had hoped to accomplish.

Her final success was in 1996, when she won the long jump at the Olympic trials and a bronze medal in the long jump at the Olympic Games, and was runner-up in the heptathlon.

Jackie Joyner-Kersee

from A Kind of Grace

One day, in 1972, when I was ten, a sign-up sheet for girls' track appeared on the bulletin board at the Community Center. "If my legs are strong enough for dancing and jumping, maybe I can run fast, too," I thought to myself. I printed my name on the first line.

A bunch of girls, including [my sisters] Debra, Angie, and me, showed up for the track team on a sunny afternoon in late May. We were dressed in T-shirts and shorts and we squinted and cupped our hands over our eyes to shield them from the sun as we looked up at our coach, Percy Harris. He explained that practice would be held every afternoon and that we had to run around the cinder track behind the Center to prepare for our races. He pointed to the area.

"All the way around there?" one girl said after she turned around to see where his finger was pointing. She turned back to Percy wearing a frown. "It's hot out here!"

224

"That's far!" another complained.

It did look like an awfully big circle, which grew wider as we got closer to it. But I kept my thoughts to myself. Momma and Daddy told us never to talk while adults were speaking. Besides, I wanted to see if I could make it all the way around. I was ready to run.

That circular track, which still exists at the back of Lincoln Park and became a fixture of my teenage years, is unconventional. It measures about 550 yards around, roughly a third of a mile. A standard track is oval-shaped and measures 400 meters, a quarter-mile. Those of us who completed the lap were panting hard by the time we reached the end. We bent over and put our hands on our knees when we finished. The other girls had stopped running and were walking. Percy said we had to run around two more times without stopping to get in a mile workout. Some of the girls mumbled and rolled their eyes. I took off around the track.

Each day, fewer and fewer girls showed up until finally the track team consisted of the three Joyner girls, two of whom were there under protest. At that point, Percy gave up the idea of forming a team. But I wanted to continue running, so he introduced me to George Ward, who coached a half-dozen girls at Franklin Elementary and brought them to Lincoln Park in the summer to practice.

"I don't know if I'm good," I said shyly when Mr. Ward said I could join his team.

"Don't worry about that. We're just having fun. If you win a ribbon, good. If not, that's okay, too," he said. I breathed a sigh of relief.

The practice sessions with Mr. Ward's group were a lot of fun. Suddenly I had six new friends. I didn't know Gwen Brown or any of the others from Franklin Elementary because I attended John Robinson Elementary and the schools were in different parts of town. Most of the others had been training with Mr. Ward for over a year and, as I would soon discover, were already very strong, fast runners.

The first race I ran for Mr. Ward was the 440-yard dash, now called the 400 meters. He lined us up opposite two bent steel poles. Then, stopwatch in hand, he walked around to the other side of the circle and stood on the board 440 yards away. From there, he yelled, "On your mark, get set, go!"

The rest of the girls charged ahead. I ran as hard as I could, but I couldn't catch them. I finished last. Once I caught my breath, I was disappointed. I couldn't believe how fast the others were!

"What can I do to get faster?" I asked Mr. Ward.

"Just keep coming to practice; you'll get better," he assured me.

I finished last or nearly last in every race that summer. But Mr. Ward stuck with me. When school resumed, he picked me up every afternoon at home in the spring and drove me to track practice at his school. I looked forward to it all day. I was eleven. I would rush home after school, cram down a few oatmeal cookies or a bag of potato chips, quickly do my geography, math, spelling, and science homework and then do my chores—or pay Debra to do them—so that I was ready when his car pulled up. I waved good-bye to Momma, who was getting home about the time I left, and hopped in Mr. Ward's car.

The practices were pressure-free, but there were rules. We weren't supposed to talk while running. But I chatted away with my new friends. Every time Mr. Ward caught me, he stopped us, pulled me out of the group, and scolded me. As punishment, he made me run in the opposite direction from the others. I didn't mind. I was so happy to be out there with the others. With a smile on my face, I ran clockwise while the others ran counterclock-wise.

One day I got sick and started throwing up while running. Mr. Ward asked me what I'd eaten. When I told him about the oatmeal cookies, he shook his head. Junk food was a no-no, he said. My punishment that time was three extra laps, all in the opposite direction. He said he wanted me to feel how eating junk food would alter my endurance. But it didn't bother me. I felt as if I could run forever. I just wasn't very fast yet.

After several more races and no ribbons, however, I became discouraged. "Am I ever going to win anything?" I asked.

He gave me a consoling pat on the back as we walked to his car. "You will if you keep working hard."

I wasn't crazy about running the 440-yard dash. But it was a challenge. I wanted to catch those other girls. My real love was jumping. But I was too shy to tell Mr. Ward. At the time I didn't know anything about the intricacies of the long jump. I just knew my legs were strong and I was a good jumper, based on my cheerleading and dancing performances.

For weeks, I watched Gwen Brown run down the long-jump track and leap into the air, like a plane taking off. I bit my lower lip as she practiced, yearning for just one chance to run down the dirt path and jump into the shallow sand. When I returned home that afternoon, I got a brainstorm. I found potato chip bags and convinced my sisters to go over to the sandbox in the park, fill the bags, and help me bring the sand back to our house. Over the next several afternoons we secretly ferried sand from the park to the front yard, where I made a small sand pit. On the days when I didn't go to practice, I hopped onto our porch railing, which was about three feet high, crouched down with my back arched and leaped into the sand. The feeling was so satisfying and so much fun, I did it over and over again for about an hour.

One afternoon after all the other girls had left practice, while I waited for Mr. Ward to drive me home, I walked over to the runway. It was nothing more than a long strip of grass, marked off with a strip of tape at one end and a shallow hole with a thin layer of sand at the other end. The sun was ready to set, but the air remained hot and thick. I was tired after running sprints and conditioning drills in the oppressive heat. But standing there, looking down the long-jump lane for the first time, I was energized. I mimicked what I had seen Gwen doing. I charged down the lane as fast as I could, planted my right foot and jumped up as high as I could. I kicked my legs out in front of me and pushed myself forward.

What a feeling! It was like flying. I stood up, content with myself and feeling daring. I smiled as I dusted the sand off my shorts and legs. Mr. Ward ran toward me. I was afraid he was going to be mad. But there was an excited look in his eyes.

"Do that again!" he shouted.

I trotted back to the starting line and repeated the process: charge, plant, push, kick, fly. His jaw dropped.

"I didn't know you could jump!" Mr. Ward said when I emerged from the sand.

"Oh, I love to jump," I said. "My legs are strong from cheerleading. I have wanted to try jumping for the longest."

"Starting tomorrow, come to the long-jump pit and I'll work with you and Gwen together," he said.

I was delighted. When he dropped me off, I skipped through the yard, bounded up the steps, and ran inside to give everybody the news.

Mr. Ward was volunteering his time to the after-school track program. In coaching young girls, he and Nino Fennoy, a teacher at Lilly Freeman Elementary who had organized a girls' squad at that school, were exploring uncharted territory and exposing themselves to criticism. No one in town had ever tried cultivating athletic interest among girls. While boys had high school and junior high teams, Little League baseball and Pop Warner football, girls in our community had no organized sports activities whatsoever.

Congress had recently passed Title IX, the federal legislation requiring public schools to give girls and boys equal opportunities to participate in athletics. Mr. Ward and Mr. Fennoy used the new law to develop opportunities for girls in sports. The combined Franklin-Freeman Elementary School team competed against other schools during the academic year. In 1974, when I was twelve, the two men organized a track squad of male and female athletes from all the schools in town that competed in summer Amateur Athletic Union (AAU) track meets. The squad was called the East St. Louis Railers.

Although I didn't realize it at the time, my participation on the Railers squad set me on a course that would lead far beyond Piggott Avenue and the Arch, into a world full of life experiences both painful and joyous.

People have always assumed I succeeded at sports because I was a natural talent. Not quite. I had talent and determination, but I needed someone to help me develop it. Nino Fennoy was that person. He encouraged me to imagine myself doing great things and worked with me to turn my fantasies into reality.

I met Mr. Fennoy on a spring day in 1973. Mr. Ward piled the girls he'd been coaching into his car and drove us to the field at Hughes Quinn Junior High, some eight blocks from my house. Every evening Mr. Fennoy worked with a group of boys and girls from Lilly Freeman Elementary at the Hughes Quinn playground. The two men had decided to divide the coaching duties of the Franklin-Freeman squad, with Mr. Ward taking the boys and Mr. Fennoy the girls.

To determine our skill level, they asked us all to run 120 yards, then circle around and run back, and repeat the drill several times. I did it easily. I still wasn't the fastest, but after almost a year of training with Mr. Ward, I had lots of stamina. I stood about five feet, five inches tall and weighed a lean 120 pounds—all arms and legs.

"What else are we going to do?" I asked the two coaches when we were done. Mr. Fennoy looked at me and smiled.

The longer I worked with him, the stronger and faster I became. But I still wasn't in the front of the pack at the end of the races—my 440 time was well over a minute. In my first race with Mr. Fennoy as my coach, I didn't finish last, but I was well back. I hoped he wouldn't be disappointed and drop me from the team.

"I tried," I said, shrugging my shoulders apologetically afterward.

He responded with a reassuring smile: "That's all I ask."

Over time, lots of girls started the Railers track program. But as training drills intensified, sessions lasted longer, and the temperature rose, many of them dropped out. A group that included Gwen Brown, Deborah Thurston, Carmen Cannon, Tina Gully, Danette, Cindy and Mona Onyemelukwe, Devlin Stamps, Pat Riggins, and I stuck it out that summer and all the seasons thereafter. We formed the core of the girls' athletic program on the south side of East St. Louis. That program included volleyball, basketball, and track squads. Most of us played two sports. I was one of the few who played all three. In summers, we competed as East St. Louis Railers. During the school year, we competed for our respective junior high teams, and later, as Lincoln Tigerettes in senior high.

Mr. Fennoy was only about five foot seven, but his ideas were lofty. The skin beneath his afro, mustache, and beard was the color of parchment and he dressed like many of the other thirtysomething men in town. But he spoke like a wise old man—a combination sociologist, philosopher, and motivational speaker. With his index finger jabbing the air and his hazel eyes staring intently at us, he peppered his speeches at team meetings with phrases like "making maximum use of minimal resources" and "the parameters of acceptable behavior."

He had a broad vision of what he wanted to accomplish through the track program. He encouraged us to work hard in practice, as well as in class. With a solid foundation in athletics and academics, he told us, the possibilities were unlimited— college scholarships, graduate school, good-paying jobs, and productive lives.

In one of his first speeches to us after practice when we were still in elementary school, he explained that success in sports could open doors for us and set us on the path to broader success. "Doing well in sports is fine. But in order to compete and get any portion of what this country has to offer, you have to have an education. You can't get a job if you can't fill out an application."

Like my parents, he stressed that there was a world beyond East St. Louis and that life in that world wouldn't be a struggle if we were properly prepared. "You have alternatives," he said. "You don't have to just be housewives. You don't have to settle for staying here."

Bibliography